TWELVE
LIES
Husbands
TELL THEIR WIVES

TWELVE LIES

Husbands
TELL THEIR WIVES

Tim & Sheila Riter

LIFE JOURNEY®
Bringing Home the Message for Life

COOK COMMUNICATIONS MINISTRIES
Colorado Springs, Colorado • Paris, Ontario
KINGSWAY COMMUNICATIONS LTD
Eastbourne, England

Life Journey® is an imprint of
Cook Communications Ministries, Colorado Springs, CO 80918
Cook Communications, Paris, Ontario
Kingsway Communications, Eastbourne, England

TWELVE LIES HUSBANDS TELL THEIR WIVES
© 2005 by Tim and Sheila Riter

First Printing, 2005
Printed in United States of America
1 2 3 4 5 6 7 8 9 10 Printing/Year 09 08 07 06 05

Cover Design: BMB Design/Scott Johnson

Library of Congress Cataloging-in-Publication Data

Riter, Tim, 1948-
   Twelve lies husbands tell their wives / Tim & Sheila Riter.
      p. cm.
   ISBN 0-7814-4133-1 (pbk.)
   1. Husbands–Religious life. 2. Marriage–Religious aspects–Christianity. I. Riter,
Sheila. II. Title.
BV4528.3.R58 2005
248.8'44–dc22
                              2004026626

With great appreciation to all those who have spoken truth into our lives, who have demonstrated integrity in their lives, and who have shared their stories with us. The line may not be fresh, but it's true: this book would have been impossible without you.

Our gratitude, respect, and thanks to:
Vickie Barton; Dwayne Benson;
Rosalie and Stan Campbell; Jerry Christensen;
Susy Flory; Teri Garcia; Guy Glimpse;
Jeannie Harmon; Fritz Moga; Curt Peterson;
Jim Price; Thelma and Herb Read; Chris Schaal;
John Southwood; Chris Houghton (counselor);
Carl Mascarella (counselor); Celebrate Recovery
at Cornerstone Community Church in
Wildomar, California; the boys at New Life; New
Hope Recovery at Canyon Lake Community
Church in Canyon Lake, California; and to many
others who wish to remain confidential.

Contents

Introduction

The Truth, the Whole Truth, and Nothing but the Truth

*Instead, speaking the truth in love, we will in
all things grow up into ... Christ.*
—Ephesians 4:15

The husband says, "I'll always love and cherish you," but after the ceremony he seems to promptly move his wife down several notches on his priority list. His gentle acts to win her heart just disappear.

The husband says, "All men look at women," but his lingering looks go far beyond a glance. He looks for opportunities to look.

The husband says, "She means nothing to me," but in truth this co-worker provides a strong temptation.

The husband says, "Somebody has to be boss around here, and God gave me that role," but she feels trampled on and ignored as a person.

The husband says, "I'll get to it next week," but next week never arrives, and she feels the brunt of his procrastination.

The husband says, "I feel great" and doesn't tell her about those nagging pains in his chest that just won't go away. She senses that he's not telling her everything, and she feels frustrated and insecure.

The husband says, "I'm not lost; I know just where we are," but she's certain he's bewildered and will drive them into a gang-infested neighborhood.

The husband says, "I have to work these long hours to support the family," but she thinks they support his workaholism more.

The husband says, "I'm sorry; I won't do that again," but she's seen the pattern and knows he just says that to silence her.

The husband says, "I know just what you need to do," but rather than a plan of action, she needs a safe haven in which to share her frustrations.

The husband says, "What you don't know know won't hurt you," so he doesn't share details of his life. But she feels shut out and separated from his world.

Wives and husbands, have you experienced some form of lying? Some form of telling less than the full truth? Perhaps it took the form of misdirection; he shaded the truth just enough to point away from reality. Perhaps he told just part of the truth; enough truth to sound good, but mixed with enough untruth to protect him.

Wives, have you become frustrated with some of the lies your husband tells you? Do you wonder why he just doesn't "tell it like it is"? Have you seen the intimacy you yearn for damaged by dishonesty and deception?

Husbands, do you wonder why you mislead your wife? Do you find it difficult to tell "the truth, the whole truth, and nothing but the truth"? Do you long for a safe environment that makes it easier to be honest? Have you become frustrated at your inability to tell the full truth to your wife?

This book and its companion, *Twelve Lies Wives Tell Their Husbands*, may provide a solution.

Wives, we'll help you learn what he really means and how to make it easier for him to be fully truthful. Husbands, we'll help you understand the impact your lack of candor can have on your wife. Then we'll help you build an environment of safe transparency. That environment gives us all the opportunity to make the most of the marriage God has placed us in.

These two books operate on the thesis that moving beyond the untruths we tell will enhance our marriages. Some untruths are humorous; some are serious. Some are direct lies;

others never say anything directly untrue, but they intentionally mislead. The more truth we tell, the closer we can get to one another. The less truth we tell, the farther apart we move. Our desire for closeness determines how honest we will be.

We realize that many wives will want to get right to the lies that their husbands tell, read them, and say, "See, I told you so! You've got to change!"

Please resist that temptation! We encourage every reader to begin by looking within and asking, "What do I do to contribute to the problem? What can I do to increase truth in our marriage?" Let's make this a time of personal change.

But, who are we? Why should you listen to anything we say? Mostly, because we've been there. We've gone through a number of struggles, most of them coming from telling partial truths or hiding things. Through painful discovery, we've learned that truth sets us free, that any form of dishonesty enslaves us. We're willing to share our journey with you, some of the mistakes we've made, and what God has done in our lives. We've both been in recovery groups. These books will come out around our twenty-sixth anniversary, and if we can make it that long, with God's help, so can you!

Our experiences include over twenty years in local church ministry, so we've seen the effects of mistruths in the lives of others. We've had to pick up the pieces that result from a lack of full honesty.

In addition, a number of friends and associates have shared their stories with us to use in these books. Generally, using a last name represents a true identity. When a first name only is used, then the identity is disguised in several significant details. Tim also teaches communications at a Christian university in our area, and he does some speaking along with writing books.

Now, before we get right into the lies, we need to lay a solid foundation on the importance of truth.

Cherish Truth

We've found that behavior follows values. Or, to say it another way, we only act on that which we truly believe. We examine the options, determine which ones best express what we view as most important, and then we act.

So, we allow untruth in our lives because we value our reputation, our finances, our comfort, or getting our way even more. That means if we want to live in truth, we must value it and the benefits it brings more than we value what untruth brings. We therefore can increase our TQ—our "truth quotient"—by increasing how much we value truth. We decide that the benefits of telling the truth outweigh the benefits of misleading people.

This can be a tough process for many of us! We've lived in various forms of lies for so long that we've become accustomed to them. Often, we don't even realize we're saying them. That's why we've been specific with the lies, to give an "Aha!" moment. "Yeah, I've said that before. And now that I think about it, I really wasn't being honest." Or, "*They* weren't being honest." Truth cuts in both directions. And although we encourage each reader to look at himself or herself rather than at others, we can all benefit from recognizing the untruths we hear.

So let's see why we should cherish truth and move away from untruth.

TRUTH REFLECTS THE FATHER

First, truth inseparably flows from the nature of all three persons that make up God. In a time of difficulty, David called on God for help and referred to him as a sheltering "rock" and a protective "fortress." Verse 5 of Psalm 31 reveals why David felt he could trust God for help: "Into your hands I commit my spirit; redeem me, O LORD, *the God of truth.*"

God the Father has truth inextricably wound up in who he is. He could no more tell an untruth than we can live on this earth without sin.

TRUTH REFLECTS THE SON

We find that same connection with the Son. On the evening before his arrest, Jesus told his disciples that he would soon be leaving. They wanted to go with him, but he had spoken of his death. They then talked about going to the Father, and

Jesus described both himself and his mission in a familiar statement: "*I am* the way and *the truth* and the life. No one comes to the Father except through me" (John 14:6). Rather than just *telling* the truth, as we may do, Jesus *is* truth. It's a part of his identity.

Truth played an equally central role in his ministry. In Matthew alone, Jesus began teaching with the phrase, "I tell you the truth" a total of thirty times. With some repetitions, in all the gospel accounts he used that phrase seventy-nine times. Why? He valued truth and wanted his hearers to be able to rest in it.

TRUTH REFLECTS THE SPIRIT

The third person of the Godhead also has truth in his character. While continuing in the subject of his imminent departure, Jesus told his followers they would benefit, since his leaving would allow the Spirit to come. Who was this Spirit, and what would he do? "But when he, *the Spirit of truth*, comes, he will *guide you into all truth*. He will not speak on his own; he will speak only what he hears, and he will tell you what is yet to come" (John 16:13). Just like with the Father and the Son, the Spirit's identity connects with truth. John defined the Spirit that way three times from 14:17–16:13.

One of the Spirit's functions is to lead us into the truth. He wants us all to have more truth in our lives, and he works to achieve that.

So when we move into truth, we move closer to God. But when we move away from truth, we move closer to the realm of Satan.

UNTRUTH REFLECTS SATAN

In a raucous encounter in John 8, Jesus made a very clear contrast between the sources of truth and untruth.

> "You belong to your father, *the devil*, and you want to carry out your father's desire. He was a murderer from the beginning, not holding to the truth, for *there is no truth in him*. When he lies, he speaks his native language, *for he is a liar*

and the father of lies. Yet because I tell the truth, you do not believe me! Can any of you prove me guilty of sin? If I am telling the truth, why don't you believe me?" (John 8:44–46)

Just as truth reflects the character and identity of God, so untruth reflects the character and identity of the devil. Think with us about those implications. Not only will untruth damage our relationships, it moves us closer to its source. Each time we allow a misperception, we make a spiritual decision. Do we wish to live in the realm of God or of Satan? Granted, we don't typically think of it in those terms, but we can't separate the behavior from its source.

Understanding the Benefits of Truth

We need to believe wholeheartedly that truth holds more benefit than untruth. Let's survey some of those benefits.

INTIMACY WITH GOD

Intimacy with God has to lead the list because there is no greater benefit, no greater goal. We're impressed with how much the apostle John dealt with the issue of truth. He presented it often in his gospel and then returned to it in the first seven verses of 2 John. To John, truth went beyond accurate statements—it encapsulated the person of God.

> The elder,
> To the chosen lady and her children, whom I
> love in the *truth*—and not I only, but also all
> who know the *truth*—because of the *truth*,
> which lives in us and will be with us forever:
> Grace, mercy and peace from God the Father
> and from Jesus Christ, the Father's Son, will be
> with us in *truth* and love.
> It has given me great joy to find some of
> your children walking in the *truth*, just as the
> Father commanded us. And now, dear lady, I am
> not writing you a new command but one we
> have had from the beginning. I ask that we love

one another. And this is love: that we walk in obedience to his commands. As you have heard from the beginning, his command is that you walk in love.

Many *deceivers*, who do not acknowledge Jesus Christ as coming in the flesh, have gone out into the world. Any such person is the *deceiver and the antichrist.*

Like his quotes of Jesus in his gospel account, John also contrasted walking in truth with deceit. And he hammered us on the point that truth and God go hand in glove. When we walk in truth (accuracy), we walk with *the* truth (the Father and the Son).

So, as we live in the fullness of truth, we increase our intimacy with God. Not a bad way to begin our pursuit of truth!

SPIRITUAL GROWTH

A commitment to truth also opens the doors to grow in our spiritual maturity. In Ephesians 4:11–16, Paul explored how our connection to others in the church allows us to grow in Christ. Verse 15 provides a vital part of creating that bond: "Instead, *speaking the truth* in love, *we will in all things grow up* into him who is the Head, that is, Christ."

Lovingly telling the truth allows us to grow. The converse: When we don't speak the truth in love, we retard our spiritual growth.

SPIRITUAL PROTECTION

We all face multitudes of temptations every day of our lives. In Ephesians 6:10–18, Paul explored the reality of that spiritual battle. He encouraged us to be strong in the Lord by using the spiritual armor that God provides. At the center of the armor lies truth: "Stand firm then, with the *belt of truth buckled around your waist*, with the breastplate of righteousness in place" (Eph. 6:14).

The belt held the armor together. Take away truth, and we lose the armor. Buckle on truth, and we take a major step in dealing with the spiritual battles we encounter. I (Tim) allowed myself to get caught up in looking at some sexually inappropriate Internet sites for about a year. And although I always knew this was wrong, in my mind I minimized the damage. Only when I accepted the truth of the damage it brought to my walk with God, my character, and my marriage could I begin to experience victory.

Truth brings spiritual protection to us and enables us to remind ourselves of reality.

FREEDOM

Jesus gave the classic verse on truth, again in the gospel of John: "To the Jews who had believed him, Jesus said, 'If you hold to my teaching, you are really my disciples. Then you will *know the truth, and the truth will set you free'*" (John 8:31-32).

In the context, Jesus talked about being free from the slavery to sin. But exactly what truth would free us? The answer has several layers. Obviously, we need to know Jesus, *the* truth. But we also need to know the truth that Jesus died to pay the penalty for our sins. We can be forgiven, but only through Jesus' death for us. And we need to know the truth that we can only access the Father through the Son (see John 14:6).

But we can't separate the truth about Jesus from our valuing truth in our daily lives. The more we live in truth, the closer we get to God. Truth allows us freedom to build more intimacy with him. It seems like that theme keeps coming back, doesn't it? Truth and closeness to God go together.

Aim for Transparency

We can describe living in the full truth as *appropriate transparency*. Transparency means we're an open book. We don't speak direct lies; we don't mislead even with truthful statements; we don't hide things that we should disclose.

But transparency needs to be appropriate, so we need to examine its two major limits.

First, does the person have a right to know? Some information is validly private. In our marriages, we don't particularly need to tell our spouses every detail of our lives before we met. I (Tim) found that mentioning I had dated a particular individual before our marriage didn't always improve things! Information we have about other people often shouldn't be disclosed without their permission.

Second, do we speak in love? Paul gave that injunction in Ephesians 4:15. If we don't speak in love, we can tell the truth but damage others. If we don't speak in love, we can tell the truth but serve our own interests at the cost of others.

We realize these two limits are loose. Exactly how we express them will vary, but we do need to ask ourselves the questions and then be certain we can answer yes to both before we proceed.

Transparency: Already a Reality with God

We're amazed at how we sometimes think we can fool others! Even more, we think we can fool God. Hebrews 4:12-13 lets us know that to God, we are already fully transparent.

> For the word of God is living and active. Sharper than any double-edged sword, it penetrates even to dividing soul and spirit, joints and marrow; it judges the thoughts and attitudes of the heart. Nothing in all creation is hidden from God's sight. Everything is uncovered and laid bare before the eyes of him to whom we must give account.

God knows our every thought, attitude, and act. Yet he still loves and accepts us. He may not always like what we do, but he does love us! We can be fully honest with God; we don't have to hide anything since he already knows it. And, knowing that he'll continue to love and accept us makes it easier to fully tell the truth to him. Our honesty with him won't hurt us.

Transparency: A Goal for Marriages

In the old *Lone Ranger* TV series, each episode began with the words, "Let's return to those thrilling days of yesteryear." For this section, let's return to the very beginning of marriage to discover God's heart for us. Genesis 2 tells us that God realized it wasn't good for his newly created man to be alone, and that none of the animals he'd created could fill the void in Adam's life. So God took a rib from the man and created the woman.

Now, notice the blueprint for marriage in verses 23-25:

> The man said, "This is now bone of my bones and flesh of my flesh; she shall be called 'woman,' for she was taken out of man." For this reason a man will leave his father and mother and be united to his wife, and they will become one flesh.
>
> The man and his wife were both naked, and they felt no shame.

First, the intimacy that both husbands and wives yearn for flows from creation—a desire to be reunited because we came from the same flesh.

Second, that yearning begins to find its fulfillment in marriage as the two become one. This oneness describes marriage at its best.

Third, marriage involves nakedness. Now, let's get figurative, not literal! Clothing keeps others from seeing physically how we really look. At this point in our lives, we wear clothing to do others a favor! But if marriage reunites us as one body, then should we hide things from our own body?

We believe our marriages should move in the direction of transparency because that best expresses God's blueprint. Will we do that perfectly? No. Does our inability to be fully transparent excuse us if we refuse that as a goal? Again, no.

In our marriages, are we "naked and without shame"? We'd like to suggest that we can't easily do the first without the second, and that comes from God himself. Marriages should be a safe place where we can grow into transparency without added guilt and insecurity. How do we combine these two?

That's important, because often when we share a failing, we face hostility and judgment. Since few of us like pain, we avoid sharing. We shade the truth. We lie. We deceive. This doesn't justify what we do—we do it in self-defense—but it damages our intimacy with God, our character, and our marriage.

God has provided a third option beyond avoidance and deceit: grace. Confronting the untruth and loving the sinner even as we hate the sin. Go back to our Hebrews passage that revealed that God knows everything about us, yet still loves and accepts us. We can be fully honest with God, knowing he won't stop loving and accepting us.

That combination of God seeing us fully and still loving us provides a pattern for how we can increase transparency in our marriages. When we know our honesty won't unduly hurt us, we can move closer to it. Realize that our honesty will often bring pain, but not as much as untruth.

That means we can help our mates be transparent. As we provide a safe harbor, we make it easier for them not to have to mislead us.

That doesn't mean we ignore sin; that doesn't mean we pretend we're not hurt by it. But we continue to love our spouses like God loves us. We continue to accept them, like God accepts us. Rather than allowing the truth to become a dividing wall, we choose to work together as a team. We realize that truth sets us free and we can then work on issues that need attention.

We realize that speaking the full truth doesn't eliminate consequences. If a husband confesses to multiple adulterous affairs, that confession doesn't clear the slate. Damage has been done, and it must be addressed and restoration attempted. Even so, the wound may be too deep for reconciliation.

But as we love and accept the other, we build an environment that encourages full honesty. That full honesty will benefit our marriages in multiple ways.

Realize also that for many of us who have allowed too much untruth to slip into our lives, who have kept things from our spouses to protect them or ourselves, that this journey to full truth is a process. We don't get instantly and totally transparent. We'll knowingly not tell the full truth at times. We'll discover areas that we may have not really understood as an issue of truth. Focus on the direction of the journey, toward truth, toward God. Don't let the failings derail you, but make them less frequent!

But as we continue to walk with truth, we'll become intoxicated with the freedom that truth brings. We'll soar in joy at the intimacy with our spouse. We'll stand in awe of the closeness we develop with God. And we'll wonder why we waited so long to pursue transparency.

Now, let's begin the journey into *Twelve Lies Husbands Tell Their Wives.*

LIE 1

I'll Always Love and Cherish You

The Truth about Making Her Feel Special

Here, these are for you," and as Dennis handed Carol the bouquet of roses, he began to win her heart. Soon, he overwhelmed her with the small touches that made her feel special. He opened the car door for her and even waited until she buckled up before driving off. He listened. They went for long walks, and he listened. He asked questions that helped her express her life's journey.

Without reservation, she gave her heart to him.

At a quiet candlelight dinner, Dennis passed her a small jewelry box and asked her to become his wife. Carol's feelings of being cherished continued to grow through their engagement.

As they stood together in church and he repeated the words of his promise, "To love, honor, and cherish until parted by death," she felt secure that this man would fulfill those vows to make her feel special.

As the years went by, Dennis progressed well at work. His company offered a promotion that provided a higher salary but required more time on the job. Faced with the increased expenses that came with their first child, he reluctantly took it. But he thrived on the new responsibilities and loved the sense of accomplishment that his new job gave. Several nights each week he brought work home, ate a rushed dinner with Carol and their baby, and then disappeared into his study to finish the paperwork.

One night each week he met with his old buddies for racquetball. He wanted to maintain the relationships he'd long had, and he knew he needed to do something to stay in decent shape. He dedicated Saturdays to a combination of home and yard projects and watching sports. On Sundays, they went to church, visited their families who lived nearby, and caught up on the sleep they'd missed with an afternoon nap.

Overall, Dennis loved his life. He provided well for his wife and daughter, his job recognized him for his efforts, and the house and yard were well kept. He never dreamed that Carol felt cheated and lied to.

The Lie

Why did Carol feel this way? In the early days, Dennis went to extra efforts to let Carol see how much he valued her. He vowed to love, honor, and cherish her. He still did, as much as he ever had. But he expressed it differently. He provided a home. He took care of her and their child. He kept up the house and yard. Of course he cherished her, but not in the way her heart yearned for.

On the Receiving End

Two years after their wedding, Carol met her best friend and maid of honor, Sharyn, for lunch.

"Sharyn, remember how we all stood up together and Dennis vowed to 'love, honor, and cherish'? That man lied. He made me feel so special back when we were dating. I was at the center of his world. We'd talk for hours, take long walks, give each other little gifts. ...

"Now I feel like an afterthought, like he just wants a companion, someone to keep house, fix dinner, and raise Samantha. I'm useful to him, but only for what I do. I don't count as a person. He doesn't have time for *me* anymore. He uses his work and friends as excuses instead of facing the truth: He doesn't like being around me.

"Just last week I fixed a nice dinner—just for the two of us. I got Mom to keep Samantha, and I had the candles out and the CDs on. But after dinner he had to go play racquetball; he'd made 'a commitment' to his friends, he said. What about his commitment to me? I just don't feel like I'm special to him anymore."

Carol expresses a common feeling of many wives: Their husbands do little to make them feel special and cherished. The women see it as a failure to fulfill the marriage vows and as a lack of integrity. That perspective comes from one of their basic needs.

A Need to be Cherished

Women generally focus more on relationships than men do. In his first video series, Dr. James Dobson observed that women tend to get their self-esteem from their marriages, while men gain theirs from work and accomplishments. That difference sets up husbands for difficulties in this area. They just don't recognize a woman's innate need to be cherished.

That's sad, because this need permeates the Bible. For women, their need for intimacy may flow from how God created men and women. In Genesis 2, God recognized the basic inadequacy of a man alone, and he took care of that lack.

> So the LORD God caused the man to fall into a deep sleep; and while he was sleeping, he took one of the man's ribs and closed up the place with flesh. Then the LORD God made a woman from the rib he had taken out of the man, and he brought her to the man.
>
> The man said, "This is now bone of my bones and flesh of my flesh; she shall be called 'woman,' for she was taken out of man." For this reason a man will leave his father and mother and be united to his wife, and they will become one flesh.
>
> The man and his wife were both naked, and they felt no shame. (Gen. 2:21-25)

To paraphrase Bible commentator Matthew Henry, God didn't take a bone from man's head that he should rule over her, nor a bone from his foot that he would trample over her. Rather, God took a rib, close to his arms that he might enfold her and close to his heart that he might cherish her. Women continue to feel a need to be held and cherished, to be reunited.

That concept continues in the Song of Songs. This remarkable love poem expresses the attitudes and actions of the wife, whom the NIV headings identify as the "beloved," and the husband, identified as the "lover." While the book serves as a metaphor for God's love of his people, it also provides a guide to marital intimacy. Husbands, we encourage you to read the entire book and see the cry of your wife's heart. But until then, read these selections and see both the wife's need to feel cherished and the husband meeting that need.

> "Like an apple tree among the trees of the forest is my lover among the young men. I delight to sit in his shade, and his fruit is sweet to my taste. He has taken me to the banquet hall, and his banner over me is love. Strengthen me with raisins, refresh me with apples, for I am faint with love. His left arm is under my head, and his right arm embraces me. ... Place me like a seal over your heart, like a seal on your arm; for love is as strong as death." (2:3-6; 8:6)

His strength brings protection to her; she feels safe. He provides her with sweets, even before the Rocky Mountain Chocolate Factory, and not just on Valentine's Day! He takes her to a nice restaurant. He floods her with love until she's ready to pass out in bliss. He provides the cuddling her heart yearns for. And she feels like he holds her close to his heart. He puts her at the center of his life, not at the fringes. To say it a different way, he cherishes her, it shows, and she knows it. So when a husband vows to cherish his wife and doesn't in the manner she needs, the wife feels lied to.

A Need to Feel Valued

Men can easily allow their own needs and desires to take priority in marriage. Someone suggested that men are self-absorbed savages only partially civilized by their wives. We wouldn't go that far, but women do have an innate need to be valued by their husbands. And when husbands don't do "those special things," wives can easily perceive their husbands as selfish. That stands in direct contradiction to how God designed marriage and established the role of the husband.

One passage we'll come back to frequently is Ephesians 5:21-33. Paul the apostle laid out God's blueprint for marriage, built on the foundation of mutual submission, each partner yielding to the deepest needs of the one they love. Husbands, read this passage carefully and note what we've italicized on how husbands should value and sacrifice for their wives.

> Submit to one another out of reverence for Christ.
>
> Wives, submit to your husbands as to the Lord. For the husband is the head of the wife as Christ is the head of the church, his body, of which he is the Savior. Now as the church submits to Christ, so also wives should submit to their husbands in everything.
>
> *Husbands, love your wives*, just as Christ loved the church and *gave himself up for her* to make her holy, cleansing her by the washing with water through the word, and to present her to himself as a radiant church, without stain or wrinkle or any other blemish, but holy and blameless. In this same way, *husbands ought to love their wives as their own bodies.* He who loves his wife loves himself. After all, no one ever hated his own body, but he feeds and cares for it, just as Christ does the church—for we are members of his body. "For this reason a man will leave his father and mother and be united to his

wife, and the two will become one flesh." This is a profound mystery—but I am talking about Christ and the church. However, each one of you also must *love his wife as he loves himself,* and the wife must respect her husband.

Husbands pattern how they treat their wives based on how Jesus treats the church, and that gives a frightening standard for men! Just as Jesus sacrificed for the church, husbands sacrifice for their wives. Doesn't our degree of sacrifice exhibit the value we hold? When husbands *don't* sacrifice, wives feel unvalued.

CONSEQUENCES OF UNMET NEEDS

Some things we desire. Fulfilled desires are nice, but not crucial. Tim desires chocolate-fudge raspberry ice cream, but he can live without it. Barely, but he can. Needs, however, are needs. Needs must be met or the organism doesn't function fully. Sheila *needs* to feel cherished and valued. If she doesn't feel that from Tim, both Sheila and the relationship will experience negative consequences.

A *lack of marriage intimacy* heads the "negative consequences" list. By that, we don't predominantly mean sexual intimacy. Mara expressed their dilemma well: "You know, our sex life is awesome. It really is. Greg cares about me; he takes his time. I love this part of our marriage, and I need it. But I can't understand why he doesn't show that consideration the rest of the time. I only feel close to him when we make love, and I need more."

Wives experience pain when husbands don't cherish them. They perceive that their husbands don't value either them or their marriage. This perception results in withdrawal. The two people begin to lead separate lives, living in the same house, but not in the same world.

Temptation increases as well. Remember that needs are needs. After counseling women for years, Sheila has learned, "A woman's home and family are her priority, and she doesn't want to look outside for her needs to be met, but she may well be driven to do so."

Please don't misunderstand: nothing excuses unfaithfulness. We can, however, push our mate into a higher level of temptation when we don't meet the needs we vowed to meet. That's the reason we've written these two books on lies we tell in our marriages: to increase the level of truth so that we can strengthen our most important relationship. And if husbands don't cherish their wives, the wives become much more vulnerable to someone else who will. That risk is unacceptable, isn't it?

Behind the Lie

If wives truly need to feel cherished, and if husbands risk serious consequences when they don't meet that need, then why in the world would men ignore this need?

Men tend to have a hunter mentality. They choose their target, determine the best strategy, and then pursue it until they catch it. At that point, the hunt is over. Mission accomplished. They can go on to other pursuits.

Single men read the books, listen to what women say, and discover by their mistakes what works and what doesn't with women. Then they do the things they must to make their "target" feel special and cherished, just as Dennis did with Carol in their early days. Once the vows have been said, though, in the eyes of men, the relationship changes. The pursuit has ended in success.

With this success, men develop a different strategy for a different type of relationship. This is marriage, not courtship! So they act as a *provider*: They feel responsible to meet the physical needs of the family. They become a *protector*: They earnestly want to defend their family against any difficulties. And they cherish the *presence*: They enjoy just being with their loved ones. Tim remembers reading the true story of a couple celebrating a milestone anniversary at a beautiful inn. They had a quiet dinner with little conversation. As they climbed the stairs to their cozy Victorian room, the husband thought, *This is a great relationship. We don't even have to talk; just being with each other is enough.*

At the same time the wife thought, *We just don't have much of a relationship. An entire meal went by with no more than twenty words exchanged between us.*

Most men who successfully provide, protect, and enjoy their wife's presence feel they're doing a pretty good job of being a husband. They're faithful to their wives; they've done what they should. They don't need to be cherished, so why should their wives? They're proud and pleased. They never dream their wives feel lied to.

Living the Truth

When dating, men like Dennis demonstrate tremendous insight when they realize what it takes to win a woman's heart. They make her feel cherished and special. But once they're married, men like Dennis demonstrate tremendous stupidity when they think women change in what they need from a relationship.

Men would do well to follow this simple principle of marriage: "We keep 'em as we won 'em." In other words, husbands need to continue to meet the needs of their wives in the same way they caused them to give their hearts.

Let's explore five steps that couples can take to live in the truth of meeting the wife's need to feel cherished.

REALIZE THE NEED

Husbands, very simply, accept this need as a *need*! Don't argue about it. Don't tell your wife that because *you* don't have this need, *she* doesn't have this need. Men and women are different! Men don't "cater to women's weaknesses" when they make the wife feel special. Each person has the right and the ability to determine his or her needs. And the need to feel cherished is an almost universal need among women. (If you don't know for sure that your wife has this need, ask her!)

Just as important, remember that you vowed to cherish her! Cherishing becomes an integrity issue. Will you keep your word?

Even so, more often than not, most men remain fairly clueless about just how to make *their* wives feel cherished and special. Men don't read minds, even though some women assume they can. Wives, your husband doesn't automatically know your deepest needs. That leads us to the next step.

ASK THEM

Several years ago, I (Tim) preached a message on loving our mates and trying to make them feel special. Driving away I felt particularly convicted to act on my sermon. I've discovered God has a way of graciously nudging me to practice what I preach! So I asked Sheila what specific acts I could do to make her feel more special. That was my mistake, to ask for *specific* acts!

An hour later, I summarized them. First, I like to be as efficient as possible. That means that when we get in the car, I buckle my seat belt, insert the key, start the car, and put it in drive almost simultaneously. I have that process down to a science! But Sheila has her purse to work with and is generally more relaxed about such things than I am. Now, I always waited until she was in the seat before I put the car in gear, but just barely. Her first request for a specific act by which I could demonstrate my love for her? The simple act of waiting until she was settled and buckled in.

My mental response? What a small issue! But from her perspective, when I didn't give her adequate time to get situated, I communicated that I cared more about getting going than about her. So that was a small change for me to make my wife feel special. And I *usually* do pretty well at it now. Usually.

Her second request demanded more of me. I have a high sense of justice, and I believe that when people do wrong they should be made aware of their actions. So when cars cut in front of me in traffic, I would brake; but I'd still allow myself to get *much* closer to their tailgate than I had to. I wanted them to know they'd done something unsafe! My actions made Sheila feel unsafe. Her second request for how I could demonstrate cherishing was not to tailgate cars that cut me off.

Inside, I reasoned that she came just as close as I did. But then I realized that when I was driving, I was in control and felt secure, but she wasn't in control and didn't feel the same sense of security. With great difficulty, I gave up playing Tim the Traffic Cop so the *real* cops could do their job. Unfortunately, in the ten years since then, not a single car has been ticketed for cutting me off. Hundreds have deserved it, but cherishing Sheila is more important to me than teaching a lesson to those drivers.

Sheila's third request was fun! And actually, it was one I already did fairly often. She wanted me to hold hands more with her and to put my arm around her shoulder when we sat next to each other in restaurants. No problem! But this story has a special twist that I'll mention in a later section.

So, husbands, if you truly do want to make your wife feel cherished and special, ask her how you can do that. And ask her to give some specific acts. Wives, don't feel like "it won't mean anything if I have to tell him," because he really is clueless here. He needs your help—he asks for your help—in meeting *your* needs. This is your big chance! From now on, he won't have nearly as many excuses for not doing it.

And wives, don't overwhelm him with a list of 632 tasks. Pick out three. Then, when several years have passed and you have him well-trained, you can add a few more. But be grateful for each step!

DO SPECIAL ACTS

Husbands, once you've asked what specific acts you can do, do them. Try to do at least two or three each week and build a habit. If you feel really courageous, ask her how well and how often you're succeeding at making her feel cherished. Remember, she's a unique individual, so her list of acts will be unique as well. Don't stop with her list, though. Most women will appreciate a number of acts, so try these just to surprise her!

Listen

Show her that you hear what she says, even if you don't agree with her words. You might try to put her thoughts into your own words to ensure you heard her correctly. Doing so can give her the sense that you truly care about her opinions and concerns. Don't automatically come back with a negative response, which can easily make her think you're not even considering what she says.

Spend Time with Her

Many husbands come home exhausted from a hard day at work and crash. They collapse in the recliner and turn on the news until dinner. Instead, ask how her day went, how she's doing. Maybe even help with dinner! (What would she do if you offered to set the table!) And, as best you can, try to have some special time each week for just the two of you. Guys, we don't mean sex here, although that may be a nice result. But get away from the home and kids. This doesn't have to be an expensive date. Stroll the mall, take in a movie, get appetizers at a restaurant, or just take a walk together.

You did that in the early days, didn't you? Like the two of us, you probably stayed up later than you should have just talking and being together. Relive those times.

Watch Your Watching of Other Women

We'll explore this more in a later section, but few things devalue a wife more than her husband looking at other women in a manner he should reserve for his wife. That look communicates the polar opposite of cherishing.

Do What You Say You'll Do

This also will be covered later, but when you put off doing what you tell your wife you'll do, you breach trust, and you discount her. Carrying out your commitments builds a safe haven for her.

Balance Interests

We each need space and our own interests, but husbands can easily allow interests outside the marriage to crowd out the relationship. We know a couple where the husband played sports four nights a week in addition to having a demanding job. The wife worked part-time and raised their four kids. Understandably, she didn't feel cherished and supported.

Build some common interests and activities. The communication theory of "Social Penetration" suggests that the number of topics that a couple talks about determines the breadth of their relationship, and how deeply they penetrate each other's personality establishes the depth. That requires time together and shared interests.

Melissa married her high school sweetheart, Tony, right after graduation and both began working. The early years of their careers demanded a lot of time, and they spent their evenings finishing off projects and taking college courses. With the great changes we all experience during our late teens and early twenties, they enjoyed exploring the new directions they took as individuals.

But within five years, they each discovered that the other had become a stranger. They'd grown in different directions, and they didn't share enough time together to even know who the other had become. Their marriage dissolved, not in anger, not in betrayal. They had just drifted too far apart.

Husbands, make sure that your wife knows you care about her development. Do the special acts.

Tell Them

This may sound contradictory, but husbands usually won't make their wives feel honored just by doing special things for them.

Remember Sheila's request that I (Tim) hold her hand or put my arm around her shoulder to let her know that I cherish her? Just the week before, we'd gone out to lunch with a group after church, and I had slipped my arm around her shoulder for at least twenty minutes. Long enough that my arm went to sleep and I had to rub it to get the circulation back into it.

Here I'd been doing it all along, and she hadn't even noticed! Rather than get self-righteous, I suggested that when I did something that made her feel loved, I would preface it by saying, "Because you're so special to me." I would help with the dishes and say, "Because you're so special." Or I would rub her aching back, again with those words.

Now, I didn't say them in jest, I didn't rub her nose in them, and I didn't say them forever. But using that phrase helped change the landscape of our relationship and gave her a vehicle to interpret my actions.

So, if you encounter the same problem we did, talk about an effective way that *you* can let your wife know that you do what you do because she's special to you.

REALIZE MEN ARE MEN

Wives, this one's for you. In all likelihood, your husband will *never* fully and completely meet your need to be cherished as you want. He's a man. So allow us to make two suggestions.

First, give him credit for the things he does *from his perspective* to cherish you. When he provides for you and the family, he does so because he cherishes you. When he protects you and the family, he does so because he cherishes you. When he's content just to bask in your presence without saying a word, he does so because he cherishes you. He will greatly appreciate it when you interpret those acts accurately—as an expression in his terms that you occupy a unique place in his life.

Second, show your appreciation for the acts he does that you've told him about. Without nagging when he seems to slip a little, remind him of how great you feel when he does those acts, and that you've missed them lately. Men respond to recognition. God hard-wired them that way, so investing yourself in some praise will give you an even better return.

Husbands, stick to your word. Cherish your wife in the ways that she desires. She'll appreciate that! And that's the truth.

Lie 2

All Men Look at Women

The Truth about Lustful Looking

The waitress came up to the table where Jeff and Carrie sat, smiled, and took their orders. As she turned away with a swing of her hips, Jeff's eyes followed her. Not the almost innate following of movement, but an intentional look. He tried to be subtle, but she looked real nice, and he couldn't avoid it. He continued to glance casually around the restaurant to keep track of her, but he kept his gaze moving so Carrie wouldn't notice.

Despite Jeff's efforts to hide the looks, Carrie saw them all—and steamed. They'd battled this issue for all four years of their marriage. She felt devalued, like Jeff cared more for his own visual pleasure than the effect his actions were having on her.

When the waitress brought their order, she had a special smile for Jeff. She'd barely walked away when Carrie unloaded. In a tight voice, barely under control, she whispered, "I can't believe you're doing this—again. You keep staring at that waitress. Don't your vows mean anything to you? You shouldn't be married; you're not ready to be faithful."

"Hey, I wasn't looking at her! I can't believe you get so touchy! Sure, I tried to be friendly to her, like I do to everyone. Carrie, I know you're insecure, but that doesn't give you the right to attack me for no reason! Why can't you just relax a little bit and not get so suspicious?

"Besides, all men look at women. God made you women attractive, and he made us to respond to what we see. We're visually stimulated. I'd never *do* anything. I'd never be unfaithful to you. It's just looking."

The Lie

Layers of deception and truth weave themselves together with this lie. Perhaps that's why men use it so often. Do all men look at women? Of course, since you can't talk to a person without looking at them. So this lie possesses the surface sheen of truth. But this answer doesn't really address the issue, so perhaps we need to go deeper.

Do all men find at least some other women attractive? We would say *probably* yes. Probably, because we can imagine some rare soul not feeling attraction to anyone but his wife, but most men would find at least some other women attractive. God created women to attract men, which allows the human race to continue. Attraction alone doesn't give us an insurmountable problem.

But let's go to the heart of the difficulty experienced by Jeff and Carrie and many other couples. Do all men look at women lustfully? No. Many do, perhaps even most. But men lie when they imply that they can't help looking at women lustfully. They lie when they excuse themselves by saying all men do it.

On the Receiving End

Jeff's denying that he looks at other women presents a major problem for Carrie. She can't fully *prove* it, although she just experienced it. She ends the conversation, but the thoughts and memories continue to swirl. Just how much *does* he look? Were some of his looks actually innocent? Did she overreact? How can they resolve this issue?

FEELINGS

A variety of emotions assail women whose husbands lie like this. *Uncertainty* may top the list. Has she gone crazy, seeing things that don't really exist? Does she misinterpret his friendliness? She really should trust him, take him at his word. Shouldn't she? Maybe the situation doesn't justify the stress and worry she brings to their marriage.

Feeling *unattractive* follows uncertainty. She's had a child or two, and she doesn't have the firm body she did when they married in their early twenties. She just can't compete with younger single women who have time to work out. She knows that variety attracts men, and they've been together for six years overall. Has boredom become a factor with Jeff?

Carrie's self-worth plummets each time she sees his gaze linger a few seconds too long. Or each time she *imagines* him doing that. Maybe she does exaggerate whatever occurs. And maybe not.

Worst of all, she feels *betrayed.* This betrayal pierces to the heart of their marriage. She doesn't feel that Jeff values her as much as the early days; he simply couldn't care about her if he keeps looking despite her protests. She knows that at one time, he valued her above all. She felt special, like Carol in the last lie. Jeff didn't look around when they were dating. So did she change, or did he? Despite her uncertainty, she knows she's not that unattractive. Something must have changed in him.

And if he'd betray her like this, would he betray her with an affair? The questions just don't stop.

RESULTS

Jeff's actions, and Carrie's emotions in response to them, have changed their marriage. She finds herself *withdrawing* from Jeff and the relationship. She feels a strong need to protect herself, since he obviously isn't going to. His looking has taken away the sense of security she needs in marriage. She just can't invest her heart in such an unsafe place.

As a result, the withdrawing *impacts other areas*. She builds other relationships and activities. The time and energy she used to put into the marriage she now uses to find safe havens: friends who love and accept her and give her emotional support, activities that she enjoys that don't necessarily include Jeff.

She begins to *lose balance* in her life. Where she once approached life with confidence, she now feels uneasy and uncertain. She's lost the sure foundation of trust in marriage, and that loss touches every aspect of her life.

And, she notices *a greater level of temptation* herself. She knows that all men *don't* look at women lustfully. Fortunately, she recognizes her emotional vulnerability and watches herself carefully. But it lurks, and her marriage frustrations have sapped her spiritual strength.

But why would Jeff, who truly loves Carrie, do these things? Why do so many husbands do the same to their wives?

Behind the Lie

Jeff immediately denied Carrie's accusations because he felt caught. He had looked, he meant to, he knew it, and he felt guilty. He also didn't feel like he could admit to it without receiving a stronger attack. So he decided that the best defense is a good offense, and he accused her of being insecure and suspicious. But again, why do so many men respond this way?

Obviously, visual stimuli attract men much more than women, and sexual stimuli fill our culture. Men can't escape the onslaught. The 2004 Super Bowl (we never can remember the Roman numerals for it, sorry!) raised a controversy over Janet Jackson's exposed breast, but the entire halftime show featured explicit sexuality. The previous year featured girls wrestling on a beer commercial that just missed qualifying as soft-core pornography. The Fox News channel often decries nudity and then puts up a scarcely smeared picture to show us how bad it is! Visual stimuli surround men; they just can't escape exposure to it.

Women tend to be more relationship oriented; they experience greater vulnerability when they feel valued, secure, and cherished. Men, however, tend to be very undiscriminating in their sexual temptation. Any attractive woman attracts their attention.

God created men to respond visually to women. Men often misuse this trait, but God did wire them this way. Even so, in Proverbs 4:25 he warned us about controlling our eyes: "Let your eyes look straight ahead, fix your gaze directly before you." He followed this in the next chapter with the dangers of adultery. But it begins with wandering eyes, and the areas of temptation extend far beyond the situation we described with Jeff and Carrie.

SOURCES OF VISUAL STIMULATION

Men face three dominant areas of temptation when it comes to visual stimulation. Some men have a vulnerability to one more than another, some get overwhelmed by all. But identifying them will help all men to understand the issue and to craft a strategy uniquely suited to them.

Just Plain Looking

Dante struggled with rubbernecking—his head moved in any direction when he saw a pretty female. He'd drive around a block to steal another glance at an attractive woman. He loved the high perch his pickup truck gave him; he could see women in other cars much more clearly.

Some men may do no more than this, but often this makes up only a part of their lustful looking.

Television

Cassandra had fallen soundly asleep by about ten, but she stirred when Raymond slipped into bed on the bad side of 2 A.M. "What's wrong? Couldn't sleep?"

"Yeah. And I wanted to watch Letterman; he had the guy on that wrote the book I just read. Then I read a little bit. Love ya."

"Me, too."

He pulled the covers over his head, but Raymond couldn't cover his guilty conscience. To avoid lying directly, he did watch Letterman—for about two minutes. Then he switched to a soft-core porn movie on one of their premium movie channels.

Cable TV has brought material into our homes that, in previous generations, a man would have had to purchase at an adult bookstore. Some men watch scrambled channels, hoping for a recognizable glimpse of bare flesh. And even broadcast TV has brought partial nudity into our homes with the Super Bowl, *NYPD Blue*, and other programs.

Jerry had carefully arranged his computer monitor in his home office to avoid any sight lines, and while making business contacts he'd surf porn channels. He'd never had a problem before, but the easy availability gave an opportunity to his curiosity, and he got hooked. Once, his wife asked him if he got porn on his email. He honestly replied he didn't and breathed a silent sigh of relief that she didn't ask if he viewed porn sites. Would he tell the truth or lie about it? He couldn't be sure, and that bothered him.

Some men struggle with one or more of these means of visual temptation, but many battle a combination. I (Tim) have had to deal with all of them. I never got involved in unfaithful actions, but I looked in each of the above manners, hurt Sheila with my behavior, and bear the scars. I've been "sexually sober" now for five years, and I deeply appreciate my sobriety. But my actions brought our marriage to a crisis. So guys, if you struggle with this temptation, and have hidden it from your wife, I can identify with you.

Living the Truth

In our opening story, Jeff felt embarrassed and guilty and wouldn't admit to the truth. We would suggest that nearly every husband involved in inappropriate looking at other women feels some degree of shame. One contributor to this book said, "In this world, we are not allowed to openly have a problem with pornography. I could admit to being an alcoholic or a drug user but not to having a desire to see women naked. I just finished reading *What's So Amazing about Grace* by Philip Yancey, and I long for a church that is more like AA: 'Hi, I'm (insert name) and I'm a lust addict.'"

Let's explore some steps that will help us acknowledge and live in the truth. Let's see how husbands can build new patterns of not looking lustfully at women. Let's discover how men can build a safe haven where they can share their struggles. With new patterns of behavior in place and a secure environment at home, husbands won't have to worry about the truth coming out, about being caught, or about having to lie and deceive.

A number of excellent books address this issue in greater detail; we'd especially recommend *Every Man's Battle* by Fred Stoeker and Steve Arterburn. We've distilled the strategy we share here from this and other books, the experience of others we know, and our own lives. Now, let's build a strategy that will allow couples to live in righteousness and truth.

UNDERSTAND LUSTFUL LOOKING

For many men, determining just what involves looking at women with lust presents a difficult challenge. Men must look at women. Many women dress to attract. Feminine beauty can tempt men, and men can't escape that temptation. Jesus gave us a principle that addresses this struggle, but it's one that we can't always understand easily.

Jesus said, "You have heard that it was said, 'Do not commit adultery.' But I tell you that anyone who *looks at a woman lustfully* has already committed adultery with her in his heart" (Matt. 5:27–28).

Let's develop a four-level understanding of lustful looking.

Not Temptation

We sometimes interpret Jesus' statement to mean that if men get tempted sexually or if they think sexual thoughts about a woman, then they've looked lustfully and have committed adultery. But temptation isn't sin. Obviously, Jesus faced temptation, yet never sinned. Hebrews 4:15 states, "For we do not have a high priest [Jesus] who is unable to sympathize with our weaknesses, but we have one who has been *tempted in every way,* just as we are—*yet was without sin.*

We hope that will take a little of the unnecessary guilt off husbands for assuming that sexual temptation is sexual sin.

Predominantly Sexual Looking

In the original language, Jesus literally said, "Everyone seeing a woman with a view to desire her. ..." Two components make up what Jesus referred to as lustful looking. Doing one or both would qualify looking as lustful.

First, when a husband looks at another woman with the thought, "I *would* do something with her if I had the chance," that's lustful looking. The only reason he doesn't act on his thought is a lack of opportunity, and there's no virtue in that!

Second, when his look focuses on the sexual—undressing her with his eyes and imagination, building fantasies that involve her—even if he wouldn't act on his thoughts, he's engaged in lustful looking. In essence he puts the woman's sexual attractiveness over her personhood.

Continued Looking

Looking doesn't rise to the level of lust when a husband sees a sexually attractive woman, recognizes that attraction, and then looks away without rubbernecking. But when he drives around the block, when he visits her desk at work more than he needs to, when he continues to think about her attractiveness, then he engages in lust.

An old Chinese proverb says that you can't stop a bird from flying over your head, but you can prevent the bird from building a nest in your hair. Husbands can't avoid facing sexual attraction and temptation; it permeates our culture. But they can avoid continuing to think about specific temptations.

Perceived Sexual Looking

Because of my (Tim's) history of looking at other women inappropriately, Sheila became very sensitive. We came to a major crisis, and I committed to change in this area. But even after that change, she sometimes interpreted innocent and non-sexual looks in light of my past behavior. When she mentioned it, we would disagree: I would proclaim my innocence, and she'd proclaim my guilt. One principle of communication states, "Perception is reality." The perception may not be accurate, but it's real to the "perceiver," and we must deal with it. Sheila *really* perceived my looking as lustful, so we had to deal with our reality.

We found that we could handle it better when she said she didn't feel "easy" about it. Using the word "easy" took the volatility out of the situation and helped us both to be less defensive. To make life better for her, I then gladly avoided whatever made her feel uneasy. That's why we encourage husbands and wives to honestly talk about this issue, so they become aware of the other's sensitivities.

Paul taught this principle in Romans 14:1 (NLT), and we'll insert a phrase from verse 2 (in italics) to best express it. "Accept Christians who *have a sensitive conscience* and don't argue with them about what they think is right or wrong."

I learned not to argue with Sheila about the accuracy of her perception. I accepted her view and changed the behavior that troubled her. So even though some looking may be harmless in a husband's opinion, if it causes trouble, then we should eliminate it for the sake of our marriage.

UNDERSTAND THE DEPTHS OF ITS WRONGNESS

During the time I (Tim) struggled with inappropriate looking—whether in person or on the Internet, I always knew it was wrong. Still, I justified it, I rationalized it, and I minimized it because I never understood the depth of its wrongness. Many Christian husbands are caught in the same struggle because lust deceives us, and we deceive ourselves and others so that we can continue with our behavior.

Amazingly, even many women will minimize it. Not long after our crisis hit, I told a female family member about it. Trying to be supportive, she said she didn't think it was that bad; her husband read some men's magazines, and it didn't bother her. I really didn't need that type of support at that time!

In our earlier story of television looking, Raymond later confessed his inappropriate viewing to his wife and that he thought he might be a lust addict. Cassandra didn't want to deal with it and encouraged him to "just stop." She assumed the problem would go away, so she never mentioned it again.

God sees it otherwise. During one period of especially difficult temptation, when I felt an almost overpowering inclination to just give in, a clear phrase came into my mind: "This is a battle for your soul." A friend, who is a pastor of a dynamic and growing church, battled Internet porn for over a year, successes mixed with failures. He finally achieved mastery when his mind heard, "This is your last chance. Once more and you're toast."

Believe us; the "fear factor" plays a significant role in building an effective strategy. But why is lustful looking so wrong?

Biblically

We've already explored Jesus' warning about lustful looking, but the greater context of another verse can add to our understanding. Many men recognize Job 31:1: "I made a covenant with my eyes not to look lustfully at a girl." When we expand that commitment made by Job to the next few verses, the importance of righteous looking becomes clearer.

> I made a covenant with my eyes not to look lust-
> fully at a girl. For what is man's lot from God
> above, his heritage from the Almighty on high?
> Is it not ruin for the wicked, disaster for those
> who do wrong? Does he not see my ways and
> count my every step? (vv. 1-4)

Let's work backwards. First, from verse 4, God sees what we do. Many men think they hide their lustful looking from their wives, their friends, even their God, but Job realized that God sees each step we make.

Second, from verses 2-3, ruin and disaster comprise the consequences of those who do wrong.

Third, from verse 1, Job places lustful looking in the category of doing wrong that can result in ruin and disaster.

Husbands, you've seen God's perspective on the wrongfulness of lustful looking. This biblical perspective can form the foundation of how we deal with this entire issue.

Relationally

Let's go back to our marriage vows, to one of the traditional lines: "and forsaking all others, be only with you, as long as we both shall live." Every ceremony includes some form of an exclusivity vow. Husbands, when you look lustfully, can you honestly claim that you're not with another woman, at least in your mind? You look at her in a manner that you vowed you would reserve only for your wife. You view other women as only their husbands should.

My (Tim's) lustful looking nearly destroyed our marriage. We've truly "gone through the fire" and been refined, but we're sure God could have accomplished the same goal without the pain I brought.

Husbands, we encourage you to read again the section, On the Receiving End, to get a sense of what your wives experience.

Obviously, if your wife catches you looking, as happened with us, she becomes aware of it. But many husbands hide at least parts of their looking. Does that mean that the relational impact doesn't exist? Not at all. Husbands get wrapped up in their own pleasure. They shut their wives out of significant areas of their lives. They tend to withdraw into fantasy and imagination. Masturbation can decrease time spent with their wives.

But the greatest damage may come in the next realm.

Spiritually

My (Tim) Internet involvement went on for nearly a year, and I went through a spiritual battle unlike anything I'd ever experienced. Again, I knew that my behavior was wrong, even though I rationalized it. But I experienced spiritual devastation in my closeness to God.

Solomon went through a great amount of sexual temptation and gave a wise warning based on his experiences. He specifically talked about adultery, but remember how Jesus linked lustful looking to the act? Solomon's basic message: Don't play with fire, or you'll get burned. "Just looking" adds an unneeded spark to the tinder of maleness.

These commands and this teaching will keep you from the immoral woman, from the smooth tongue of an adulterous woman. *Don't lust for her beauty*. Don't let her coyness seduce you.

For a prostitute will bring you to poverty, and sleeping with another man's wife may cost you your very life. *Can a man scoop fire into his lap and not be burned?* Can he walk on hot coals and not blister his feet? So it is with the man who sleeps with another man's wife. He who embraces her will not go unpunished.

Excuses might be found for a thief who steals because he is starving. But if he is caught, he will be fined seven times as much as he stole, even if it means selling everything in his house to pay it back.

But the man who commits adultery is an utter fool, for *he destroys his own soul.* (Prov. 6:24-32 NLT)

We're convinced that husbands can't continue "just looking" and thrive in their walk with God. The holiness of God can't coexist with continuing known sin. With every step we take toward sin, we move further from God, according to Isaiah 59:2: "But your iniquities have separated you from your God; your sins have hidden his face from you, so that he will not hear."

Defining temptation in spiritual terms helps many husbands resist temptation. We simply ask ourselves, "Do I want a closer look at this woman, or do I want a closer walk with God? I can't have both."

UNDERSTAND THE DYNAMICS

Do you remember the old wives' prescription, "Feed a cold, starve a fever?" In the above passage, Solomon compared lustful looking to a fever. The more we feed it, the hotter it gets. How do we ratchet down the temperature of the temptation? By understanding that the more input we allow, the stronger the desire gets.

Men often think that once they marry, frequent sex with their wives will decrease the level of their desire. Not! Like a muscle, exercise merely increases the strength! That means, for husbands susceptible to looking lustfully at other women, the more they look, the stronger the drive gets.

BUILD A STRATEGY

Because most men who look inappropriately have become masters of minimization, we need to build a strategy that is much more radical than we seem to need. Trust us on this, Tim's an expert. A friend of ours got enmeshed in Internet porn and inappropriate behavior, and as a result, even attended a lengthy seminar led by Christian counselors. But in conversation later, he seemed both to minimize the behavior and rely on "trusting in God's grace." He didn't develop an accountability partner; he didn't build a habit of going to any form of support meeting. Within six months, his behavior escalated into work-related sexual harassment and he lost both his job and his marriage. Why? He tried to take it easy on himself and continued in his behavior because God's grace always brought forgiveness.

Now, let's explore a five-step strategy on building new patterns that can bring victory over lustful looking.

Create a New Mind-set

We begin with changing our attitudes about the activity. Romans 8:5 states, "Those who live according to the sinful nature have their minds set on what that nature desires; but those who live in accordance with the Spirit have their minds set on what the Spirit desires."

Said another way, when we face a temptation, we remind ourselves of our new values. Sometimes, physical objects can help. Tim typed out a phrase, printed it, and taped it to his computer monitor: "A new year, a new man; in a battle for the soul."

Stoeker and Arterburn, in *Every Man's Battle*, encourage men to focus on a key verse that we can recall at difficult times. Many discover that Job 31:1 provides a quick boost of spiritual strength: "I made a covenant with my eyes not to look lustfully at a girl."

Find a Safe Haven

To successfully deal with *any* sin pattern, we need a safe haven where we can honestly tell about our battles, grieve over our losses, and receive personal acceptance without acceptance of the sin. Ponder James 5:16: "Therefore confess your sins to each other and pray for each other so that you may be healed. The prayer of a righteous man is powerful and effective."

Mutual sharing of our struggles, in an environment where we can be scrupulously honest and open, brings power and healing. We suggest that your spouse may not be the best source in the beginning. Find a group of men where you can tell the hard truth. Many have discovered twelve-step support groups to be effective, whether Christian-based groups, such as Celebrate Recovery, or secular groups like Sexaholics Anonymous.

You may find a time when you need to bring your wife into the equation as well. In our early days, Sheila's wounds went so deep that we couldn't talk much about the specifics. But as Tim built more of a history of dealing with his sin, we've been able to share openly.

Identify Vulnerabilities

Each husband will discover that different environments, activities, relationships, or conditions will increase vulnerability. For Tim, being tired or sick greatly decreased his resistance. So husbands need to play a little bit of detective and determine where they struggle the most, what makes them most susceptible.

Once we identify our weakest times, we can proceed to the next step.

Minimize Temptations

Remember Jesus' strategy for avoiding sin in Matthew 6:13: "And lead us not into temptation." For spiritual success, we need to get as far from temptation as we can. That may mean ending some relationships. A friend of Tim's stopped getting Internet access at home. Others use an Internet service provider that comes with a filter, like American Family Online. Covenant Eyes will email a record of the Internet sites you visit to an accountability partner.

Other men we know have only basic television and don't subscribe to cable. Your personal strategy depends on your unique vulnerabilities, so fine-tune it to your situation.

No matter how complete our plan, we can't eliminate all visual temptations in our culture. When we can't avoid temptation, Stoeker and Arterburn recommend "bouncing" our eyes away from the target. As soon as we identify something that leads us down the road to lustful thinking (and for most guys, that can happen very quickly!), we bounce our eyes away. Look at a woman's face instead of her chest. Look at the cars ahead in the road instead of the pretty jogger on the sidewalk. On occasion, graphic pop-ups hit Tim's screen, so he covers the screen with his left hand while his right moves the cursor to close the pop-up. "Bounce" whenever you need to in whatever way you can!

Rebound

These steps will work. We've distilled them from both experts and our experience. But we seriously doubt that each husband who reads this book will use the strategy and never look lustfully again. Make sure you don't make the same mistake Dan did.

After years of lustful looking at other women and more recently at porn sites on the Internet, Dan got into a recovery program and made some great progress. His confidence level grew, and he thought he had this problem licked. But not long after receiving his one-year pin for sexual sobriety, work got frustrating, his wife began complaining, and he found himself viewing porn again.

Devastation swept over him; all his efforts had gone for nothing. He embarked on a porn binge, feeling that he'd already blown it. Shame overwhelmed him for several months until he dragged himself to a meeting. Slowly, he got back on track and learned that nearly everyone "falls off the wagon" at least once.

The apostle John knew the tension between yearning for righteousness yet never attaining it. "If we claim to be without sin, we deceive ourselves and the truth is not in us. If we confess our sins, he is faithful and just and will forgive us our sins and purify us from all unrighteousness" (1 John 1:8–9).

In talking to followers of Jesus, John assured them they would still sin. But rather than descending into a downward spiral of shame and embarrassment, we can choose to confess our failures to God and to others and thus bring spiritual restoration. Please don't take this as an excuse to fall off the wagon! But don't allow a fall to kill you, either. Satan can bring more damage to us after the sin than in the sin itself if we don't rebound.

So for all husbands who use the excuse that "All men look at women" to justify your behavior, you need to stop. You *can* change your behavior. You can live, and look, without fearing that the truth becomes known. And that's the truth.

Lie 3

She Means Nothing to Me
The Truth about Attraction

During premarital counseling, the counselor led Tony and Debbie into a discussion about how much of their previous sexual experiences they should talk about with each other. Both had limited experience and thought it wise to leave it at that. Neither would identify people they'd been intimate with. They resolved to "let the past stay in the past."

Debbie assumed those women had left Tony's life, and Tony was happy to allow that assumption. They just never discussed this subject. About six months after their wedding, Debbie went through the desk while paying bills and found a packet of letters in the back of a drawer. Each was addressed to Tony, each from Joan, each postmarked from several years before their marriage.

Curiosity caused her to open a letter, and she discovered that Joan, a co-worker of Tony's, had provided his first sexual experience. The romantic part of the relationship lasted only a month, but they remained as friends, and they still worked together. And Joan had attended their wedding.

Tony came home to an icy wife. "I found the letters."

A momentary look of confusion spread over his face, then a single word escaped. "Joan?"

Her glare confirmed his fear. A long pause, then, "I think you have something to tell me, don't you?"

"She means nothing to me. Years ago, we got carried away at a convention. We both agreed that our friendship and our working relationship were more important than our physical attraction. And I knew it was wrong. We stopped it. Now we work together. That's it."

"Tony, she's come to dinner in our *home*. She attended our *wedding*. Don't give me that 'she doesn't mean anything to me' line!"

"Debbie, we talked about this in premarital. We said we wouldn't bring up what we'd done before, or who we'd done it with."

"But I didn't know she was still in your life! I didn't know she was at our wedding! I didn't know you kept her letters! Don't you think that changes things just a little?"

"No, it *doesn't* change things. Joan and I haven't touched each other in four years. I married *you*, not her. I haven't been unfaithful to you. Honestly, she means nothing to me."

"Then why did you keep her letters?"

The Lie

This lie takes us a step deeper than the last. That one focused on looking, which can exclude any kind of relationship. Here, the husband faces a temptation to get involved with another person. Or, he has gotten involved either in an affair of the heart—he has an emotional or romantic connection with another woman of the type he should only have with his wife—or an affair of the body, which can range from inappropriate touching to intercourse. Whatever the form, this lie represents a deep and genuine threat to the marriage.

But what makes the statement "she means nothing to me" a lie? In Tony's case, he hadn't been fully honest with his wife, since Joan still played a role in his life. They had a history and saw each other every day. Although no romance now bloomed between them, they pressed the dry rose of romance between the pages of their memories. Also, he hadn't been fully honest with himself either; that's why he kept the letters. He truly loved Debbie and would never think of cheating on her. But he did remember the special moments he and Joan shared, and he kept the letters in order to keep the memories alive.

When husbands deny—to others or to themselves—that they feel an attraction to getting involved with another woman, they lie.

On the Receiving End

Wives may experience many of the same feelings they did with the last lie, but the emotions go both deeper and broader, since attraction represents a much greater threat to the marriage than looking does.

Debbie felt lied to and betrayed. Her dad had repeatedly cheated on her mom, and Debbie carried that fear into her marriage. Tony kept up the friendship with Joan because he saw no intrinsic problem, but he hid the extent of their previous relationship in part because he knew of Debbie's insecurity. She felt much more insecure when she discovered Joan's intimate history with her husband.

Debbie began to wonder if Tony compared her to Joan. He only saw Joan at her best; he saw Debbie with bed hair, morning mouth, and flannel pajamas. Did he compare them sexually? Did Joan do more to please him? Did he find her more attractive physically? Still single, Joan did put a lot of care into her personal appearance. Debbie even wondered if she'd had plastic surgery.

Discovering the letters made her question her values and whether Tony shared them. She deeply valued honesty, and yet she believed Tony had lied. She deeply valued fidelity, and yet she saw Tony's continuation of his friendship with Joan as a threat to their marriage. She deeply valued her husband, but she thought he placed his friendship with Joan above her.

Behind the Lie

As an extrovert, Tony valued a number of friendships that went back years. He just enjoyed people, and he didn't need romance to do that. So he carefully established strong boundaries to keep his relationships with women on the platonic level. His relationship with Joan had been appropriate for four years, and he had no concerns about the sexual involvement recurring. So he couldn't understand why Debbie wanted him to end the relationship. He felt mistrusted and innocent of any wrongdoing. But although he knew nothing would happen, that he didn't want anything to happen, he still remembered. The letters reminded him of a very special time in his life. He couldn't quite let go of the memories. And he wanted to protect these special secrets.

Beyond Tony's story, we find two issues hiding behind the lie. Why do men feel an attraction to other women? And why do they hide it?

WHY THEY'RE ATTRACTED

Some men feel attracted to other women because of unmet needs in their marriages. Unmet needs increase the vulnerability of a husband. Unmet needs may be relational—someone who cares, who respects them, who listens. They can also be sexual—the frequency, acts, or absence of satisfying sex. Emotional intimacy may head the list. When the two have grown in different directions, they share little of their deeper selves with each other.

Again, we want to stress that if our spouse doesn't meet our needs, we don't have the freedom to go out and meet our needs in other relationships. But unmet needs do make husbands more vulnerable.

Men seem to have an innate desire for *variety*, but men aren't known for their discrimination. Almost any attractive woman can grab their attention—along with many who'd never have a shot at Miss America! Visual stimulation impacts men much more than it does women.

And God did create men with a need for variety. Unfortunately, most men think that means a variety of women instead of a variety of experiences exploring the depths of just one woman.

Needs for ego reinforcement also make men more vulnerable. Why do young men brag about their sexual "conquests"? To establish their masculinity, to show they're smooth, to build their egos. Think with us about the concept of "the trophy wife." The man marries his high school sweetheart, they build a career and family together, then in their forties, when they've reached some success, he dumps her for a young, attractive, firm body. Why? To show he's arrived, that he can still attract younger women.

These reasons don't excuse anything, but the better we understand them, the better we can deal with the lie.

WHY THEY HIDE IT

But why do men hide relationships they're tempted with? Why don't they share these struggles with their wives so they can work together?

Many times, husbands don't reveal their attraction to another woman because they fear their wives will become fearful and insecure. Tony validly had that concern. Sometimes the men don't feel safe enough; they know they'll face accusations. The husband anticipates an attack and expects the issue to bring division rather than unity.

Rather than facing his wife's fears or biting words, he doesn't say anything. And if she asks, he denies it, saying, "She means nothing to me." In actuality, he's battling the attraction—maybe he's even shared it with a friend—but he doesn't feel safe enough to share it with his wife.

When the lie "she means nothing to me" refers to a relationship that has already gone beyond appropriate, he has even more reasons to not tell the truth. By getting involved, at whatever level, he's moved away from the marriage. He's allowed a possible threat to become a real danger to his marriage. He teeters on the edge of determining what direction to go relationally. Will he end the marriage and pursue the new woman? Will he try to maintain both? Will he end the unfaithfulness? Will he end the specific relationship and continue to pursue other women?

Typically, husbands only come clean when they've made a decision either to end the marriage or to end the unfaithfulness and restore their marriage. Guilt, self-preservation, or the desire to maintain the unfaithfulness all combine to cause them to hide their involvement.

Living the Truth

Let there be no doubt: The above reasons for attraction and hiding an attraction to other women never justify the lie. But they form the foundation for developing a plan of attack so that couples can live in the truth. Let's explore five steps to reach truthful living.

REMEMBER YOUR VOWS

Husbands promise faithfulness to their wives when they marry. Remember the traditional phrase, "*forsaking all others*, be only with her, as long as you both shall live"? In marriage, we put our integrity on the line by promising that we'll only allow romantic or sexual thoughts and acts with our wives. So we begin our strategy by remembering that we've already promised fidelity, which, not coincidentally, has tremendous importance to God. Read Malachi 2:14-15.

> The LORD is acting as the witness between you and the wife of your youth, because you have *broken faith with her*, though she is your partner, the wife of your marriage covenant.
> Has not *the LORD* made them one? In flesh and spirit they are his. And why one? Because he was seeking godly offspring. So guard yourself in your spirit, and *do not break faith with the wife of your youth*.

Apart from our relationship with Christ, no commitment has more importance than our marriage vows. When we break those promises, we reveal something about our integrity. We demonstrate by our behavior that we'll only keep our commitments when it's convenient, or when doing so yields what we want.

Husbands, in building a strategy to live in truth, we encourage you to think frequently about what you promised to your wife: faithfulness.

MOVE TOWARD HONESTY

A commitment to move in the direction of scrupulous honesty makes up the second step. The introduction covered this principle, but review this simple encouragement: "Therefore each of you must put off falsehood and *speak truthfully* to his neighbor, for we are all *members of one body*" (Eph. 4:25).

Paul addressed members of a local church with his encouragement to speak truthfully because they all belonged to the body of Christ. Married couples have an even deeper body connection, being one flesh. Just as if you stub your big toe, your entire body experiences the effect, what one spouse does will impact the other. Debbie expressed it: "Anyone in his life was by default in my life. I felt it was unfair to expect me to have any woman in our lives that had previously been intimate with my now husband."

A commitment to honesty touches four areas. First, we need honesty with *ourselves*. Husbands, carefully examine the relationships you have with other women. That includes neighbors, co-workers, church relationships, and extended family members. Some will count as totally platonic, both emotionally and physically. With others, you might feel an attraction, a desire to get closer. Honestly examine the current and potential risk of each. And, please, err on the side of caution.

Several years ago, a noted Christian leader allowed a platonic friendship to grow into adultery, a temptation he'd never struggled with before. His conclusion? "An unguarded strength is a double weakness." Restated, we can get blindsided if we don't keep our guard up.

When you feel an attraction—or even the chance of it— admit it. Acknowledge it to yourself. You can't build a battle strategy if you don't admit the battle exists.

Second, we need honesty with *God*. We've found this step opens up great reservoirs of strength in facing temptation. God already knows we face the temptation, so admitting it to him means we get on the same page. He doesn't have to work to convict us of the truth; we know it. That knowledge allows us to move farther along.

Third, we need honesty with *others*, particularly a trusted and wise male friend, a person with whom we can be scrupulously honest and transparent, who won't minimize the sin but will still love and accept us. Openness with one person will bring spiritual accountability into our lives, will show us the freedom of transparency, and will open up spiritual strength for us. "Therefore *confess your sins to each other* and pray for each other so that you may be healed. The prayer of a righteous man is powerful and effective" (James 5:16).

Last, we need honesty with our *spouse*. The degree of truth-telling may vary from one couple to the next, based on their unique background and relationship. Some men could easily say, "Honey, I'm finding that Marsha from our Bible study might be a problem. Can you stay with me when she's around?" A husband's willingness to be that straightforward with his wife empowers them to work together to fight against a threat to their marriage. Other couples may find the above example to be beyond their level of comfort, but remember that we want to move in the direction of honesty. Find the exact way that best works for you.

BE ALERT

Being alert expands what we talked about in moving toward honesty with ourselves. Men especially, with their visual sensitivity, need to evaluate just about all relationships for their "attraction potential." Even though we may *think* a certain relationship is safe, affairs typically involve friends. Safe friends.

Slipping into an inappropriate relationship looks like fun, like pleasure. We focus on the good side and ignore the dangers. The book of Proverbs makes these dangers vivid!

> For the lips of an adulteress *drip honey*, and her
> speech is smoother than oil; but in the end she is
> *bitter* as gall, *sharp* as a double-edged sword. Her
> feet go down to *death;* her steps lead straight to

the grave. She gives no thought to the way of life; her paths are crooked, but she knows it not. Now then, my sons, listen to me; do not turn aside from what I say. Keep to a path far from her, do not go near the door of her house. (5:3-8)

Adultery appears attractive, but we need to be alert to the damage it brings. That means we have to carefully analyze our relationships and look for a variety of problems.

Real Problems

Real problems arise when we feel a desire to get closer to a person of the opposite sex in a romantic, relational, or sexual manner. The problem may have grown to actual involvement or it may involve just the desire for emotional or physical gratification. Either way, we cannot deny the threat. Husbands need rigorous self-honesty when looking for real problems. They may want to delude themselves, but they need to yearn for the truth.

Potential Problems

Husbands also need to look out for potential problems. Tony ignored this step. Once a couple has had intercourse, a special bond exists. The Bible uses the same term to describe marriage and intercourse: two becoming one. The act of sex changes the relationship. Does that mean that two people who have experienced sexual intimacy cannot be "just friends"? No, but they need a continual awareness that their vulnerability has increased.

Like the Christian leader we mentioned earlier, the couple may think their new "friendly" relationship maintains solid boundaries, but they need to know that "an unguarded strength is a double weakness."

Potential problems come in a great variety of roles and places, so husbands must develop an alert attitude to any danger that might arise.

Perceived Problems

Perceived problems arise when the wife feels threatened by an outside relationship the husband has, even if it truly is platonic. Debbie experienced this type of insecurity. She knew Tony had no current involvement, but because of her own family background, she just couldn't handle the relationship. Tony didn't want to hurt Joan, and he couldn't understand why Debbie objected. He saw no potential problem, and he wanted to ignore the perceived problem.

In cases like this, husbands need to yield to their wives' greater sensitivity. Paul gave that principle in Romans 15:1: "We who are strong ought to bear with the failings of the weak and not to please ourselves." Even though Tony didn't think his friendship with Joan would ever cross the boundaries again, his greater commitment to his wife should have trumped his friendship with a co-worker.

PROTECT YOUR PRECIOUS

Along with most of the world, we loved The Lord of the Rings movies, especially watching the Smeagol/Gollum character. He allowed the desire for power to take over his life, and although he often battled the desire, he finally gave in. Why did he cling to the ring of power so tightly? He called it "my precious." That ring had ultimate value to him, and he eventually sacrificed his identity and his life for it.

Husbands, you'll build an effective strategy for living in the truth when your wife becomes "your precious." Short only of your commitment to God, value your wife above all—above career, above self-pleasure, above your hobbies, and above your own interests. With that value in place, you'll embark on a godly journey. Let's look at some steps to protect your precious.

A Time to Run

The story of Joseph has long intrigued both of us. One reason we respect him comes from his response to sexual temptation. Genesis 39 tells how he rose to the position of running his master's entire house and that he was "well built and handsome." His master's wife started hitting on him, repeatedly and blatantly. At first he reasoned with her, but one day, when everyone had left the house, she grabbed him by the cloak.

At this point, Joseph apparently gave up on reasoning. Why? Reading into the situation a little, we believe it was because he felt some measure of sexual attraction. He ran, leaving his cloak in her hands. That "evidence" led to a charge of attempted rape, and Joseph landed in prison.

He lost the respect of his master; he lost his freedom; he lost his reputation; he lost pretty much all he had—except his integrity. And to him, his integrity was his most valuable possession.

Husbands, when you examine your relationships and find some real, potential, or perceived problems, be willing to run—even though running may carry a high cost. Others may question your judgment. You may lose a job. You may lose some friendships. But the rewards of valuing "your precious" above all others will far outweigh any cost.

Build Some Hedges

On the rural farms of Bible times, farmers would often plant thorny hedges around their gardens to keep out pests. We can do the same in our marriages. Long before he wrote the Left Behind series, Jerry Jenkins wrote a book called *Loving Your Marriage Enough to Protect It* (Moody Press). In it, Jerry suggested that husbands build "hedges"—rules of behavior— that are designed to protect their marriages. He offered his six hedges as examples, and we summarize them here. Think of them as wise guidelines, not as legalistic requirements.

1. Whenever possible, avoid time alone with any woman who is not your wife. Why? Obviously, if we never get alone with a woman we can't easily have an affair! But we also minimize the personal interaction that builds attraction, which can set the stage for more involvement. Invite a third person to your meeting, lunch, or whatever. When a last-minute change of plans makes this impossible, make sure your wife is the first to know and that she hears it from you!

2. Be careful about touching. Previous generations never touched a member of the opposite sex, except maybe to shake hands. Hugging and touching have increased, and that can be good and healthy. But exercising some care in *how* we touch and *whom* we touch can help us avoid the road to sexual temptation. A lot of college students now practice a "side hug" to avoid some of the body contact that men can interpret as erotic. Touching an arm or shoulder can express care, unless we let the touch linger. Extending your hand immediately can help answer the sometimes awkward question of whether or not a hug is expected.

3. Compliment carefully, and never flatter. Words have power because they carry meaning. However, people can give different meaning to the same words. Saying, "You really look hot," while perhaps given innocently by the man, can take the relationship to another level when the woman interprets it in a noninnocent manner. Proverbs 7:21 (NLT) talks about the power of words: "So she seduced him with her pretty speech. With her flattery she enticed him."

Here's a quick test to distinguish between flattery and a compliment: Who benefits? Flattery benefits the giver; compliments benefit the receiver. If we say something to advance our cause, to make the person more favorable to us, then we've moved from complimenting to flattering. And flattery can lead to dangerous consequences.

4. Never flirt, even in jest. More than once, I (Tim) have joked around in a friendly fashion and had it taken as flirting. I didn't intend it and never had a clue about how my comments were perceived, until another person—often Sheila—pointed out how the other received it. She called it correctly, and I'm really trying to avoid anything in conversation that might be misinterpreted.

Why should we avoid flirting? Flirting brings romance and sexuality into the conversation. People begin to interpret what we say in light of romantic possibilities, even if we don't intend to communicate those options. Why should we play with talk about the type of relationship that dishonors God and our mate?

5. Remember your vows. We suggest you do this on two different occasions. First, think about them when you face a temptation. I (Tim) have found that my wedding ring works miracles. If I sense a woman coming on to me, I touch my ring to remind myself that I'm committed to Sheila and no one else. Sometimes I even flash it just a little. Not that it's flashy, but the ring does carry a message!

Second, tell your wife, in creative ways, that she's stuck with you. She *expects* stuff like that on anniversaries and Valentine's Day, so surprise her on days with no special meaning. You might want to practice your CPR first, though, in case the initial shock gives her a heart attack.

6. Keep dating. Jerry said this differently, to spend both quality and quantity time together, which is good. But make some of that romance time for just the two of you. Get a babysitter if needed, see a movie, or just spend the evening at home cuddling and see what develops. Make sure you take time to talk about the events of your lives.

The more we meet our needs in marriage, the less temptation we'll face to get needs met outside of marriage.

Well, husbands, we've tackled probably the biggest lie of all: unfaithfulness, the temptation to stray. We've seen the importance of fidelity. Husbands can remain faithful—in act and in heart. And that's the truth.

Lie 4

Someone Has to Be the Boss Around Here, and God Gave Me the Role
The Truth about Headship

Gary and Pam met in their church's high school youth group and felt an instant connection. They gravitated toward each other at group events and discovered they could talk for hours. They began double dating when Pam turned sixteen, and they went solo not long after. Her parents appreciated Gary's giving spirit, and he didn't push their boundaries. She got home on time, he came to the door, and both valued sexual purity.

They attended different colleges, but not too far apart, so they kept the relationship going, just not as frequently. Everyone expected them to marry after graduation, and no one was disappointed.

Then the young married group at the church went to a conference led by a national ministry, known for its strong teaching on headship by the husband. Gary took seriously the responsibility of leading his family spiritually. He'd never really thought of the issue much before, so he studied the verses they mentioned and committed to become the priest of his family.

As time passed, Gary's leadership slowly grew into domination. When their home church blew up in a political fight, Gary chose their new one. He did listen to Pam's concerns—

kind of. But he wasn't concerned that she never quite felt comfortable at the new church.

Five years into their marriage, Pam suggested an idea to Gary. "You know, honey, we don't have any kids, and it looks like we might not ever. Since I already have my teaching credentials, I talked to the principal at the Christian school at church, and they could use me part-time, two days a week, in the elementary grades.

"We'd have a little more money, and maybe we could give a little more to that orphanage down in Mexico. But most of all, I'd like to know that I'm using my education and contributing something to others, and to my own life as well. What do you think?"

"Absolutely not. I'm the breadwinner here, remember? That's part of the responsibility God gave *me*. I wouldn't be the man God wants if I allowed you to do that. And we still might have kids; you know we haven't stopped trying! Besides, you should feel fulfilled as my wife. That should be enough."

Knowing she'd lost the battle, Pam gave it up and never mentioned it again. But the yearning never left her heart.

Four more years passed, and she woke up one morning a little queasy. Thinking about it, she realized she'd missed her last two periods. Her typical irregularity had kept her from really noticing. She tightly harnessed her emotions as she went to the store and purchased an early pregnancy test. Positive.

A smile escaped, but she called her doctor and made an appointment. Another positive. She met Gary with a smile when he returned from work, silently handed him the results, then together they exploded in joy.

Pam began to dream of the pregnancy. Her parents lived in the same town, and she anticipated sharing the pregnancy with her mom. They could decorate the baby's room together, plan the showers, and Mom could join her and Gary in the delivery room. Life couldn't be better.

A few weeks later, Gary came home with a big smile and plans for dinner at a nice restaurant. They chitchatted over the meal, and as the waitress brought the fudge cake, Gary announced, "Pam, I have some *really* good news. Remember that project I proposed about expanding our sales force into new regions? They went for it! And they want me to oversee the southeast region. They offered me the job today, and I accepted. "We're looking at a salary *increase* of over $50,000. They even pay all our relocation costs."

"Relocation? What are you saying?"

"Isn't it obvious? The southeast headquarters will be in Alabama, so the company's paying us to move. We don't even have to pack; professionals come in, box our stuff, pack it, ship it, and unpack it. We just have to walk through the door!"

"But Gary, I'm pregnant! Mom lives here in town. All our friends live here. This is *not* a good time to move!"

"Honey, I know what you're saying. But I've thought and prayed about this quite a bit. This opportunity can give us financial security. We can give more to God's work. It puts me on the fast track for more promotions at work. You'll never have to think about teaching again to bring in a little more money."

"Gary, I wish you'd talked this over with me before you took the job. This impacts us as a family, and I'm part of the family! You need to take my concerns into account."

"Pam, I have. Again, I've thought about this a lot. Someone had to make this decision. Yes, we disagree, but someone has to be boss around here, and God gave me that role. The decision is final. We're moving to Alabama. And I expect you to submit on this issue. Remember, God made me the head of this house."

The Lie

Marriage roles have experienced great change over the last forty years or so. Contemporary marriages generally focus more on equal sharing, discussion, and coming to mutual agreement. Traditional roles tend to focus on the husband as head of the house, sometimes as the priest of the family. As such, the husband bears responsibility for the spiritual well-being of the entire family and makes the decisions. Gary comes from this camp, which may seem more biblical than contemporary.

However, this position focuses on authority as the key component of headship, and it misses the biblical pattern. It ignores mutual submission, it ignores husbands sacrificing for their wives, and Christ did both for the church.

When husbands claim that God made them "the boss," they don't speak the truth.

On the Receiving End

A week after the restaurant discussion, Pam met her childhood friend Lucinda at a local coffee house. She sipped her iced latte, and a sigh escaped. "You know, I always wanted to be a godly wife, a godly woman. I wanted a partnership, an equal partnership. But Gary's changed since we got married.

"Back in high school, before a date he'd ask where I wanted to go. He considered me, my feelings, my desires. That's why I married him! But now I feel suffocated; he's so domineering. He doesn't seem to respect me as my own person, as an adult. I can't believe we're moving halfway across the country, and he didn't even mention the possibility until it was a done deal!"

"Oh, Pam, you must be furious!"

"I am, and I'm starting to resent him, too. I oppose anything he suggests just to show I have some backbone. He seems to want a nice, sweet Stepford wife; someone who'll agree with him no matter what, with a smile and a grateful heart. I can hardly stand it anymore!"

"Hey, he can't be all bad."

"No, he can be generous and helpful. He surprises me that way sometimes. But he does what *he* wants to do for me. He doesn't really consider my feelings and desires. And this job is just the latest. He wants to rip me from my parents and my friends, and he won't let me use my education."

Pam paused, thoughtful. "You know, I probably wouldn't feel so upset if I thought he viewed me as a partner in all this, if he honestly listened to my concerns. But he doesn't. Maybe I won't go to Alabama."

When husbands insist on their authority and dominate, when they don't carefully listen to their wives, wives typically experience the feelings that Pam did. They feel discounted and devalued as a person. They come to believe that their value consists only in the services they provide to the husband. He wants a bed partner, a cook, a housekeeper, a mother, but not a wife.

In this situation, wives often develop an attitude of passive aggression. They resist the husband in a variety of subtle manners designed to thwart him without overt conflict. They've learned they can't win an open conflict, so they become masters of disguising the battles. They may run late or delay household tasks, just to assert their individuality and personal power.

Some wives even turn off to God when the husband continually insists that God made him the boss. What kind of God would discount someone so much?

As a result, the distance grows between the husband and wife. They miss the pattern of one flesh that God designed as the heart of marriage.

Behind the Lie

As we mentioned a little earlier, the tremendous change in marriage roles has unsettled many. One stream in our culture moves toward a more equal basis and away from the traditional expectations. In reaction, another stream moves toward the more traditional roles. And many just don't have a clue. Couples develop a working pattern with elements of both but with little biblical underpinning.

Until about fifty years ago, the Judeo-Christian ethic combined with traditional cultural roles to give most couples a fairly clear idea of what to expect from husbands and wives. The husband served as the head, the breadwinner. He made the major decisions.

The wife's role encompassed the homemaker and child raiser. She supported her husband, recognizing his headship even as she learned how to become the neck that turned the head.

These general descriptions may appear a touch simplistic, but they represent a basically accurate picture. While these traditional roles didn't always match the biblical pattern, they came closer than many of the newer perceptions of roles.

World War II began the change; women filled the factories as the men went off to war. With that, a chink appeared in the armor of husband as sole provider. But the change really hit its stride in the Sixties with the sexual revolution, birth control, feminism, and an emphasis on equal rights for women.

Now, some marriage counselors assert that wives provide the primary leadership role in many families. Many husbands have become passive, valuing peace and harmony above leadership.

Other families react to the changing roles of our culture by moving back more strongly toward male headship. Our story of Gary and Pam expresses this philosophy. Other lies in this area include the belief that no innate differences exist between males and females, just what we teach little boys and girls. Others acknowledge gender differences but won't extend that into the roles in marriage. They practice very egalitarian roles; each couple can develop the roles that work best for them. The growing numbers of house husbands expresses this.

All of these misconceptions thrive when we misunderstand the different roles God established for husbands and wives. In this chapter, we'll explore some biblical truths about headship. God does describe the husband as "head" of the family; we'll see what he means by that. God does encourage wives to "submit" to that headship. We'll cover that in our companion book, *Twelve Lies Wives Tell Their Husbands*, so if you have both books, try to read these two together.

Living the Truth

Before we live the truth, we need to understand the truth. When we know the truth, then we can identify the lies and misconceptions that we encounter. Uncovering the lies will allow us to express God's truth in our marriages.

HEADSHIP CONFIRMED

God clearly provides the concept of the husband as head of the marriage. "For *the husband is the head of the wife* as

Christ is the head of the church, his body, of which he is the Savior. Now as the church submits to Christ, so also wives should submit to their husbands in everything" (Eph. 5:23-24).

Many have built huge theologies on husbandly headship from those two verses. Their reasoning goes that since God gave the leadership role to husbands, then wives must do whatever they ask. Some have even suggested that if the husband commands the wife to act immorally, she should go ahead and do it. She's not responsible, since her "head" commanded her. He bears the sin, she does not. This extreme example reflects the impact of sin on the concept of headship.

HEADSHIP DEFILED

Let's go back to the original pattern for marriage that flows from the very creation of people. God's design for us came in Genesis 1:26: "Let us make man in our image, in our likeness, and let them rule over the fish of the sea and the birds of the air, over the livestock, over all the earth, and over all the creatures that move along the ground." So men and women together represent the image and likeness of God, and they were given a responsibility to steward the rest of his creation. That sounds good, and it gets better!

Verse 28 tells husbands and wives to "be fruitful and increase in number; fill the earth and subdue it." A tough task, but someone has to do it!

What progress report did God give himself for this work? "God saw all that he had made, and it was very good" (v. 31).

Then Genesis 2 gives a flashback that amplifies the creation of men and women. Adam had been created, but he needed a companion, someone to fill up the empty spaces in his life. God then created Eve, and in Genesis 2:24-25 he gave the blueprint for marriage: "For this reason a man will leave his father and mother and be united to his wife, and they will become one flesh. The man and his wife were both naked, and they felt no shame."

Let's summarize the main points God gives for marriage.

1. We leave other family relationships and make our marriage the primary one.

2. The joining of a husband and wife can be so close that they can be described as one.

3. Nakedness, or transparency and vulnerability, should mark the marriage.

4. Shame need not be a part of marriage.

What a great pattern! But do we really base our marriages on it? Too often, we cling to our parents and don't give primacy to our mates. Too often, our lives intersect, but we wouldn't dare claim that we've achieved oneness. Too often, we hide things from our mates. (Isn't that why we wrote and you're reading this book?) And too often, we feel shame because of our imperfections, because we don't love one another unconditionally.

Why have we fallen so far short? Sin has continued to warp the entire concept of headship, and that distortion began with sin's first entry. Adam and Eve invited sin into the world, and we've each invited it to stay. After the Fall, God pronounced curses on the serpent and the ground, and he gave consequences to Adam and Eve that affected the oneness that should have existed in marriage.

Let's examine these consequences.

Shame

Shame entered the world when the couple realized their nakedness and their sin. "Then the eyes of both of them were opened, and *they realized they were naked;* so they sewed fig leaves together and made coverings for themselves" (Gen. 3:7).

Did they not know they wore nothing? Were they the original emperor who had no clothing? No, with the opening of their eyes, they realized they'd done something wrong. God wasn't there then, but they seemed to know he might see them. Their nakedness no longer was appropriate.

Ever since, husbands and wives have had to deal with their sin, their embarrassment, the sense that someone will judge them. We tend to hide not only our physical nakedness, but our emotional and spiritual nakedness as well. We hesitate to reveal our real selves.

Blame

Blame came along with guilt and shame. We prefer not to own our actions. Rather than admit we did wrong, we try to place the blame on others. When God confronted Adam, Adam tried to shift the blame first to Eve, then to God himself. "The man said, 'The woman you put here with me—she gave me some fruit from the tree, and I ate it'" (Gen. 3:12). "God, she did it. But remember, you gave her to me, so it's your fault, too. If she hadn't come along, everything would be fine." Husbands haven't changed much in several thousand years. They do something wrong, feel shame about it, then when they get caught, they lie or deceive to cover it up.

Eve likewise tried to blame someone else, so she chose the only one who hadn't yet been blamed: "The serpent deceived me, and I ate" (3:13). In essence, she said, "It's not my fault. I got tricked; I didn't really know what I was doing."

Desire for Domination

The wife's desire to dominate the husband entered the world. Husbandly headship and wifely submission work well in a perfect environment like the Garden of Eden. They both became more difficult when sin entered the equation, which occurred when God said to Eve, "Your *desire* will be for your husband, and he will rule over you" (3:16).

Husbands typically interpret that word *desire* to mean the wife will sexually yearn for the husband, which they certainly don't view as a curse! Sorry, guys, that's not the meaning. Remember, things got worse with the curse, not better!

Rather, it means that wives will desire to dominate their husbands. Notice the contrast between the two phrases, her desire and his ruling. Strong's dictionary gives one definition of desire as "the craving ... of a beast to devour." Doesn't that work against headship? Absolutely. The wives will rebel at submission. They'll want to be boss. But this desire merely sets up a battle with the fourth consequence of sin.

Husbands Rule

We watched a movie with our grandkids recently and heard a great line, obviously given by a cat: "Cats rule, dogs drool." Everyone wants to rule—including husbands! Not only will they want to, God says they will! (See v. 16.)

Rather than exercising a sacrificial love for his wife, a husband will resist his wife's domination by exerting his own. And Adam didn't wait long to begin his rule. Look at verse 20: *"Adam named his wife Eve, because she would become the mother of all the living."*

Not long before, in Genesis 2:19, Adam did something similar. "Now the LORD God had formed out of the ground all the beasts of the field and all the birds of the air. He brought them to the man to see what he would name them; and whatever the man called each living creature, that was its name." Naming represented an act of authority, and in naming his wife Eve, Adam exercised authority over her.

We see how sin warped the original pattern of marriage into a battle for authority. Now let's see what God meant for headship.

HEADSHIP REVEALED

The word *head* can mean many things. It can refer to the front: Walk to the *head* of the classroom. *Head* can refer to a source: The *head* of the Mississippi River is in Minnesota. It can refer to authority: He's the *head* of the company. It can also refer to more distasteful things. All sailors know what happens in the *head* of a ship! (Landlubbers know it as a restroom.) So before husbands claim headship too quickly, they better know what they want!

We want to learn God's concept of *head*, so we must go to the greater context of where we first found headship mentioned. Ephesians 5:23, which expresses the headship of the husband, is part of a greater principle.

Ephesians 5:18 begins with a command, an imperative, to "be filled with the Spirit." Then the writer, Paul, gave four participles that explain how to be filled with the Spirit. The New King James Version expresses them clearly:

❖ "*speaking* to one another in psalms and hymns and spiritual songs (v. 19)

❖ "*singing* and making melody in your heart to the Lord" (v. 19)

❖ "*giving* thanks always for all things to God the Father in the name of our Lord Jesus Christ" (v. 20)

❖ "*submitting* to one another in the fear of God" (v. 21)

To rephrase, we allow the Spirit to fill us when we fill our lives with spiritual conversation, with spiritual singing, with giving thanks, and with submitting to one another. The last point provides the foundation for headship and submission in marriage. All Christians are to submit to other Christians. If husbands and wives are Christians, they're expected to submit to each other!

Thankfully, Paul went on to tell us how to submit in several different situations:

❖ 5:22-24 tells wives how to submit to their husbands

❖ 5:25-31 tells husbands how to submit to their wives

❖ 6:1-3 tells children how to submit to their parents

❖ 6:4 tells parents how to submit to their children

❖ 6:5-8 tells employees how to submit to their employers

❖ 6:9 tells employers how to submit to their employees

Allow us to outline this passage to let the greater context shine clearly.

I. Be filled with the Spirit
- A. Speaking spiritually
- B. Singing spiritually
- C. Giving thanks
- D. Submitting to all
    1. Wives submit to husbands
    2. Husbands submit to wives
    3. Children submit to parents
    4. Parents submit to children
    5. Employees submit to employers
    6. Employers submit to employees

Forgive the length, but we put it there so we can all see that headship is in the context of submission, which is in the context of being filled with the Spirit. Now, let's pull some conclusions about headship from the verses about husbands.

Jesus Patterns Husbandly Headship

Husbands sometimes develop their understanding of headship from the culture, which provides a variety of conflicting messages. Even within Christian circles, any given church may present a different slant on the subject. Husbands can also get their information from their own fallenness and carnality, which encourages them to get their own way by whatever means necessary.

But if husbands claim headship, they must pattern it after Jesus. "For the husband is the head of his wife, *as also Christ is the head of his body, the church*" (Eph. 5:23 NLT).

The rest of the section details how Christ acted as head, which gives husbands a clear picture of how to act as head in their marriages.

Sacrifice Merits Headship

Husbands tend to think that their headship comes from their position as husband. Gary's belief that God gave husbands the role typifies this belief. Yet we don't see this pattern with

Jesus. He didn't claim headship over the church because of his deity. Husbands, don't attempt this at home.

Rather, Jesus' sacrifice set the stage for his headship, a principle that husbands tend to ignore. "For the husband is head of the wife, as also *Christ is head of the church*; and He is the Savior of the body.... Husbands, love your wives, just as Christ also loved the church and *gave Himself for her*" (Eph. 5:23-25 NKJV).

We just can't escape the link between headship and sacrifice. Husbands, this is a husband talking right here. We simply can't exert any authority without expressing any sacrifice. God links those two concepts in the person of Jesus.

On the big things, husbands sacrifice gladly. Most husbands would literally give their lives to protect their wives. But will they sacrifice their preferences, their comfort, and their leisure time for the sake of their wives? Perhaps wives find submission difficult because their husbands try to use headship as a tool to get their own way. Perhaps—just perhaps—wives could submit better if husbands would sacrifice better.

Headship Develops the Wife

Along with many husbands, Gary used headship in an unbalanced manner. Since Jesus gave us the pattern, what goal did he use headship for? Jesus' desire was for his church to be holy. "Husbands, love your wives, just as Christ loved the church and gave himself up for her *to make her holy*, cleansing her by the washing with water through the word, and to present her to himself as a radiant church, without stain or wrinkle or any other blemish, but holy and blameless" (Eph. 5:25-27).

Husbands, headship carries with it responsibility: You must do your best to help your wife grow into the fullness of the person God designed her to become. Jesus sacrificed his own comfort and pleasure that the church might be "holy and blameless." He wanted the church to become all it was meant to be. Yet many wives complain of feeling stifled, of feeling that they have to submerge their personality, gifts, and interests for their husbands. Pam felt like that. Unless husbands will do for their wives what Jesus did for the church, they have no right to demand that their wives submit. Again, Christ didn't say to the church, "Okay now, first you submit to me, and then I'll help you." He took the initiative.

Every relationship needs a person with primary responsibility. As heads, husbands should help the family develop spiritually. They do that by setting an example of sacrificing—first for God, second for their wives. They do the right thing first, without making their actions conditional upon the wives doing the right thing.

Husbands set the spiritual direction of the family; they insure that the family honors God. They don't have to come up with all the ideas. If they did, they wouldn't be allowing the others to fully develop their creativity. But they make sure that the family continues to move in the right spiritual direction.

Decision-making provides one of the greatest areas of conflict in marriage. Ideally, in mutual submission, make decisions together. Talk them over, work them out, pray about them, and try to come to conclusions that both of you can live with. And, for those times when a decision must be made, and you can't agree, let the head decide. However, he must decide from a posture of sacrifice and a desire to help his wife and family develop. Gary missed this last point. He showed no willingness to sacrifice his dreams, but he did show a willingness to sacrifice Pam's. That's not headship, but ruling.

PRACTICAL HEADSHIP

Let's look at two practical tips for how husbands can act as the biblical head of the house.

Love Your Wife

In an earlier chapter, we talked about how Tim asked Sheila for some practical ways to demonstrate his love for her. Guys, we encourage you to do the same. Paul told us to love our wives as we love our own bodies. Do the things for her that you'd do for yourself. If you like a night out with the guys, don't complain if she wants a night out with the girls. Encourage her to pursue her interests, and then give her the help she needs to make it happen. Verbally express your love for her more frequently. Most wives appreciate hearing the actual words "I love you." Your speaking lets them know you cherish them. But make sure that your actions back up the words, or they'll come across as hollow and meaningless.

Develop Your Wife

Try to make her life easier. I (Tim) recently taught a writing class to graduate ministry students, and one wrote a hilarious article describing the four children she had at home: two sons, a daughter, and a husband. She could chuckle and laugh, but her husband made life more difficult for her, and it was actually more sad than funny. Guys, do the small things. How about taking your dishes to the sink and actually rinsing them and putting them in the dishwasher? How about hanging up your wet towel? Could you even consider burping with your mouth closed? Personally, I'm working on trying to remember to turn my socks right side out before putting them in the dirty clothes hamper. It's a battle, but why should I increase her workload unnecessarily?

We've seen a lot of husbands spend time at the gym developing their bodies. Husbands, make a similar commitment to developing your wives. Not that you work out with them at the gym, either! (Then again, why not?) But identify the unique gifts and abilities your wife has, and encourage her to use them. Make it possible for her to pursue them. Don't quench her the way Gary did with Pam's teaching gift.

Spiritually, help her by setting a solid example of a person who loves Jesus and wants to follow him. Take the initiative on spiritual issues, even on simple things like helping get the kids ready for church on Sunday morning (or Saturday evening!). Don't frustrate her by acting selfishly.

Husbands, become a Christlike head, one who loves and sacrifices for his beloved. Replace being the boss with being a sacrificial husband, and you'll discover some changes—good changes—in your wife. And that's the truth.

Lie 5

I'll Get to It Next Week
The Truth about Procrastination

"Jason, I need you to get that painting done in our guest room today. Mom's coming to visit next month, and I'd really like to have it finished by then. Okay?"

"Traci, I hear what you're saying. But today is already pretty well filled up. Then we have church tomorrow, and our small-group potluck in the evening. Tell you what, I'll get to it next week."

"Why have I grown to hate that phrase? Whenever I ask you to do something, you say, 'I'll get to it next week.' Face it; you just don't want to do it, so you keep postponing it."

This pattern of her asking and him procrastinating typified Traci and Jason's marriage. Planning ahead for room for their "future" kids to play, they paid a premium for their oversized lot of almost a quarter acre. Four years later, it featured dirt, dirt, and more dirt, accented with some scattered weeds. Jason's construction company boomed, but he frequently worked six days a week.

Traci loved their large house and nurtured dreams of what she could do with it. They hadn't quite anticipated the cost of window coverings, landscaping, and all the extras that came with creating a new home. Still, she developed a two-page "honey-do" list of projects for Jason. Each project he completed seemed to remind Traci of several more things he could do.

After a year in the house, their first child, a son, came along, followed by a daughter two years later. As the children grew, so also did Traci's frustration with the unfinished backyard. She frequently voiced her feelings, until Jason could no longer bear her nagging. So one Saturday found Jason knocking down some of the larger weeds and beginning a trench for a retaining wall on one side of the yard. After a couple of hours he came into the house, grabbed a glass of ice water, and said he had to meet the guys from their small group for the church-league softball game.

"Jason, I thought you were going to finish the trench today."

"Yeah, I hoped so, but I did all I could. The guys are counting on me for the game. I'll get to it next week. I'll do it, honest. Next week."

Four years later, Jason finished the backyard. But the honey-do list continued to grow, along with Traci's frustration. She'd ask him to do something, and he'd respond, "I'll get to it next week."

Sometimes he did. Sometimes he didn't.

The Lie

Jason said he'd get to it next week as a way to avoid doing the job. Although he didn't mind working hard, he wanted some time that he could take charge of, and he felt that, if he let her, Traci would take up all the time he had. He knew that the intervening week would often provide more reasons for delay. Perhaps a church function, perhaps visiting family, or a family activity. He used these excuses to avoid coming right out and saying he didn't want to do the task. He knew Traci got frustrated, but he had learned early on that if he could just put her off, she wouldn't confront him.

In truth, Jason didn't particularly plan on doing anything next week; he just wanted to get Traci off his back.

On the Receiving End

Like most women, Traci cherished her home. She liked to build a nest, one that she felt comfortable in and that reflected her personality. Not merely a shelter from the elements, her home provided a sense of security against the world. And she had a nice decorating touch. She knew what she wanted her home to look and feel like.

Combining her creativity and a good sense of organization, she soon developed a huge list of projects for the home. Repainting, wallpapering, wainscoting, new window coverings were only the beginning. She wanted an herb garden outside, a lot of lawn for the kids to play in, and a built-in barbecue for the times they hosted the small-group meetings in the summer.

She couldn't understand why Jason didn't value their home as deeply as she did. He seemed to be content with a much more vanilla-style home. She yearned for raspberry fudge ripple.

As her frustration grew, she took Jason's procrastination personally, as neglect of her. If he truly cared for her, how could he ignore tasks that had such importance to her? Her attitude and his inaction began to influence their marriage. She felt she had to nag to get him to do anything. But the more she nagged, the more he resented it, and the more he kept putting things off. So she got more frustrated, nagged more, and he resisted more. Traci and Jason both felt trapped in a terrible downward spiral. She knew she'd feel more content and secure when the house and yard were completed, and he knew he'd feel better if she'd just leave him alone. But it seemed like that glorious day would never arrive.

Behind the Lie

Why do husbands often put their wives off with a line like "I'll get to it next week"? Four primary reasons exist.

OTHER INTERESTS

Typically, a husband doesn't value the home as much as his wife does. To a wife, the home provides the center of her world.

A place for the family, a refuge, her personal creative palette. A man doesn't view the home in such a central manner. Yes, his home composes a large part of the mosaic of his life, but to him, it's just one piece. He doesn't see it as a reflection of who his is. Television counselor/host Dr. Phil tells men, "Don't mess with the nest. If mama ain't happy, ain't nobody happy."

Jason was pretty sure he maintained a good balance between home needs and establishing his career. On the job, he was in the midst of refining some procedures that should pay off nicely over the next ten years. He also maintained a good set of friendships. A couple of nights each month he'd get with friends, and he often played softball on Saturdays with the guys from church. Sundays mostly went to church activities, and he didn't want to give up all his weekend time to honey-do lists. He wanted some time just to relax, watch sports, and hang.

FEELING OVERWHELMED

Traci's huge honey-do list overwhelmed Jason; he felt he'd never be able to finish. Like many men, he didn't shine at multi-tasking. He could focus well on one thing, but don't even ask him to listen while he was working on something! All his attention went to the task at hand. And in his opinion, there were way too many tasks at hand!

FEELING UNAPPRECIATED

At a primal level, men need to receive appreciation and respect for what they do, and Jason felt that Traci didn't appreciate what he did. Each completed job led to two more, and she focused on what he hadn't done rather than on what he had. Just a year before, he had repainted the guest room, and it turned out quite nicely. But Traci wanted to change the accent colors on the window coverings, which required another coat of paint. Now she wanted it done again for her mom's visit, when it looked perfectly fine, thank you very much!

Jason felt that if his wife valued what he did, she wouldn't keep asking him to make changes.

CONTROL MECHANISM

Deep down, almost subconsciously, Jason knew he procrastinated because Traci pushed so much. Resisting gave him a sense of control in his home life. He didn't want to be a milquetoast husband who merely said "yes, dear" to all she wanted. He felt he needed to protect his masculinity.

To him, always going along with her meant that he abdicated his own desires and his ability to make decisions about how to spend his time. Of course, he'd never admit that to Traci; that would only cause a bigger fight.

Living the Truth

This issue of the wife's to-do list and the husband's procrastination causes tremendous conflict in a marriage, and the struggle comes from the core of both people. Women value their home and want their husbands to share this value; husbands feel unappreciated and overwhelmed. So let's explore four steps that could help us navigate this minefield.

RECOGNIZE THE DIFFERENCES

As we've stated, women definitely view the home differently than men. In recent years, many have read the description of the good wife in Proverbs 31 and stressed her role in business, which certainly surpasses the traditional role of women to "just" run the household. Among her tasks, she involves herself with international commerce ("She is like the merchant ships, bringing her food from afar" v. 14); she runs her own business on the side ("She considers a field and buys it; out of her earnings she plants a vineyard" v. 16); she makes money through trading ("She sees that her trading is profitable" v. 18); she gets involved in charity work outside the home ("She opens her arms to the poor and extends her hands to the needy" v. 20); and she has a home manufacturing business ("She makes linen garments and sells them, and supplies the merchants with sashes" v. 24).

In reading through what she does, we identified fourteen tasks. Beyond her outside work, ten of those tasks directly relate to the home. She selects the raw materials and makes clothing for her family (vv. 13, 21); she acquires food and prepares it for her family and servants (vv. 14–15); she weaves in the home (v. 19); she oversees having bedding and linens (v. 24); she oversees the entire household (v. 27); and she raises the children (v. 28).

What a woman! Yes, she's involved outside the home in a variety of business ventures, but she gives primacy to what she does in the home.

Husbands, realize your wife sees your home as the heart of her life. Yes, you like and value your home as well. But you two look at it a bit differently. That doesn't mean that one view is right and the other wrong; they're just different. Keep that truth in mind as we go along.

Submit to Her Needs

We talked about the need for mutual submission in our last chapter (Eph. 5:21). Men, make a commitment to yield to this very important need of your mate. Begin with a willingness to change your attitude. Don't automatically resist her requests. Don't continually put it off till next week. Develop a desire to help her achieve her dreams. Remember Dr. Phil's line: "When mama's happy, everybody's happy."

Work Diligently

Guys, we'll provide a balance to this in the next section, but once you've committed to understanding and meeting your wife's needs on the home front, apply the same motivation to your home that you use for working hard to build a career.

Let's explore how principles from Proverbs about diligence apply to the home front.

First, "Do not love sleep or you will grow poor; stay awake and you will have food to spare" (20:13). Or, realize that Saturdays aren't designed for you to sleep and relax all day. Yes, we need some of that, but we can overdo it, too!

Next, "Finish your outdoor work and get your fields ready; after that, build your house" (24:27). Or, prioritize what you do. Determine what's most important long-term, and focus on that.

We suggest that family trumps both career and leisure. Why? "Better a meal of vegetables where there is love than a fattened calf with hatred" (15:17). Or, express to your wife how you love her by taking on the honey-do list. When you value what she values, you show you value her.

When you share her priorities, you avoid building resentment in her, which can happen if you continually procrastinate. "An offended brother [or wife!] is more unyielding than a fortified city, and disputes are like the barred gates of a citadel" (18:19).

DEVELOP A WIN/WIN STRATEGY

We can easily go to extremes. Part of Jason would love to come home and vegetate for the weekend—watch some sports, play a little, go to church, and relax a lot. Traci, though, could keep him busy four days a week with projects from her creative mind. Neither of these would lead to a happy spouse.

We suggest that couples try some constructive communication to work out a strategy that both will feel good about. This concept comes from Romans 14:19: "Let us therefore make every effort to do what leads to peace and to mutual edification." Homes need peace. Both husbands and wives need to be built up and have their needs met. So let's move the discussion away from a battle where each wants to get his or her way, to a resolution that benefits both.

Peaceful resolution will only occur when we genuinely care about the needs of our spouse and balance his or her needs with our own. Listen to Paul's advice: "Do nothing out of *selfish ambition* or vain conceit, but in humility consider others better than yourselves. Each of you should look not only to your own interests, but also to *the interests of others*" (Phil. 2:3-4).

Traci has a genuine need for home jobs to be completed and not postponed. Jason has a genuine need to relax and carry out other interests. When they both approach the situation with a concern for the other's needs and not just their own, then they can build a win/win strategy.

With Philippians 2:3-4 as our foundation, let's see how that might be done.

Share Your Desires and Frustrations

Sit down with each other when you both feel rested and unstressed, with no kids around and no distractions. Then, talk about what changes you'd like to see. Begin with some of the ideas you have about what you'd like to see get done, along with how much time you think could be given to each project.

To clear the air and to aid in understanding each other, express your frustrations without attacking the other. Try to focus on what you feel in response to specific statements or actions.

Traci might say, "When you tell me you'll 'get around to it next week,' I feel ignored, like you're just trying to shut me up. And when you don't do it the next week, I feel even more unvalued, like you don't care about me."

Jason might say, "When I get this huge honey-do list, I feel overwhelmed. It's just too much to think about at one time. And when you nag at me, I feel unvalued, like you value me only for the jobs I do, not for me."

This discussion can be dangerous, so be gentle and understanding with each other. Focus on trying to understand where your spouse is coming from, what he or she is feeling and thinking. Practice the Philippians principle of having concern for the other person's interests, even above your own.

Make Changes Through Love

Out of your concern for your spouse, seriously consider her viewpoint. Try to get inside his head. Not that you necessarily agree, but strive for understanding and empathy. And make a decision to change what *you've* done in the past, rather than primarily focusing on changes the other person needs to make.

Traci might commit to nagging less or not putting thirty-five tasks on the honey-do list. Jason might commit to spending more time on the various projects or maybe even to letting her determine what he'll work on and when.

Work Out a Plan

Together, develop a *list of the projects* that you need to complete, and then prioritize them as you work with each other. Mix in small and large items, critical jobs and preferences, maintenance and new projects. Make sure you can get a sense of making progress.

Next, develop some *time parameters*. When we faced this issue, we agreed that Tim would give his Saturdays to home jobs, both maintenance and new projects. Sheila agreed that she'd be satisfied with whatever got done within that time frame.

Obviously, things come up. We've worked it out that if a family event creates a conflict, then we go with the family event and try to find some other time to make up for the work at home. Our latest struggle has been with our new church football league that plays Saturday mornings. Since Tim hasn't yet acknowledged that he isn't still in his twenties, he signed up. But he really can't call football a family event, so he makes up for his missed work time on Sunday afternoon or during the week.

On Saturdays (when he's not playing football), Tim attacks the list and has wiped out one project entirely. Wives, lists on smaller pieces of paper are always appreciated! Also, husbands appreciate it when you take the time to update, revise, and maybe even reorder those lists.

Every family will work this out in a different manner, because each family differs. But when we each strive to empathize with the other, we have the platform to resolve the problems.

The next suggestion involves the wives. *Express appreciation*. Husbands need to know that their wives think of them as a hero, as an accomplished worker. Wives, the investment of compliments and appreciation will pay relational dividends beyond your imagination. When you focus on what he *has* done, you'll discover that he does more. Husbands, *keep it up*. Don't allow this to become another tactic to get your wives off your backs! Some husbands will jump into the plan, work hard for a month or so, and then gradually slack off. They didn't intend for this to be a "forever-and-ever-amen" type of thing, just a temporary restraining order to minimize nagging.

This behavior certainly doesn't express a desire to look after the wives' interests like their own. So, men, look deep within and check your motives. Remember, "husbands ought to love their wives as their own bodies. He who loves his wife loves himself" (Eph. 5:28).

Sometimes, men slack off because old habits re-emerge before new ones can develop strength. They don't knowingly choose to stop; they just slide to a halt. In this case, a gentle wifely reminder will usually get the process back on track.

Wives possess a genuine need for their husbands to work in the house and yard, to complete some of the projects that are important to them. And when husbands do more, then the wives discover that they want to do more for their husbands. Everybody wins!

Husbands have a genuine need for leisure and to relax. So work together, as members of one another. Don't procrastinate. Don't nag. When we do this, we discover partnership at its best, both working together so Satan can't get a foothold and tear us apart. Your marriage will be better for it. And that's the truth.

Lie 6

I Feel Great

The Truth about Health Concerns

Honey, are you sure this is the best time to start an MBA program? After all, you've got a lot on your plate. That new software program at work sucks up your time already. And you look pretty tired."

"Karen, I just have to get that MBA. I'm stuck at my current level at work without it. And the job will never get less stressful. When I finish this project, they'll have another one for me. Besides, I feel great. I think my tiredness comes from fighting off that cold that so many people have. I'm only thirty-nine, still in my prime."

Rick, a classic, driven Type A, went on to enter the MBA program at Pepperdine University, one of the best-respected in the region. He drove nearly 100 miles to the satellite campus and then back home after the class ended at 10 P.M. Homework ate up another six hours or so each week, which caused him to complete much of it after the kids had gone to bed.

His health began to show signs of neglect. Karen finally got him to fit in a physical and asked him about the results when he returned home.

"Well, the doc said I ought to watch my weight. I hadn't realized it, but I'm up fifteen pounds since I started school. I was sure the dry cleaners were shrinking my pants! But everybody gains a little weight in middle age. No biggie."

"Anything else? You've been eating a lot of fast food with your traveling. How's the cholesterol?"

"Not bad, about 210. I should watch that, too, get more exercise, and eat better. But honestly, I feel great. I don't know why he's so concerned."

Rick finished the MBA program but didn't slow the pace of his life. Now in his mid forties, he knew he ought to exercise, so he started playing softball with the church team once a week.

He came back from one game pretty tired, huffing and puffing a bit. "Man, those young guys get quicker all the time!" He rubbed his left shoulder; he must have pulled it swinging the bat.

Karen noticed Rick's shortness of breath and his shoulder discomfort and said, "Rick, those two symptoms can indicate a heart problem. I'm really concerned. We better call the doctor."

"Hey, don't stress over it. I just had to run more today; I guess middle age is catching up with me."

"Honey, let's not take this lightly. We need to call the doctor."

"No, I feel fine. Just the normal aches and pains."

Two weeks later, Rick had a mild heart attack. He got out of the hospital after a few days, but the doctor took him to the tool shed. "Rick, you have a serious problem here. You got lucky this time, but your cholesterol has continued to climb. Your last test had it at 250. And when I told you to exercise, I didn't mean to play sports just once a week—that's worse than doing nothing. Your body isn't twenty-five anymore, and you're not in good enough shape to stress it that way.

"I want you to get a membership at the gym, start taking this cholesterol medication, and lose some weight."

Rick followed doctor's orders religiously—for a few months. But he missed the adrenaline rush of his hectic lifestyle, and he began slipping. Too many projects at work kept him from the gym, and Karen noticed. She always noticed.

"Rick, I'm really concerned. You haven't kept up with what the doctor wanted, and you're tired all the time. I love you, and I don't want to lose you."

"Lose me? That won't happen. I feel great, I really do. Sure, I feel some aches and pains, but not much."

At only forty-eight, the big one hit. Rick spent weeks in cardiac intensive care; the doctor didn't think he'd pull through. He finally returned home, but he was unable to work. His MBA benefited him not at all. The company put him on disability, but it barely paid the bills.

Even with insurance, the bills devastated them financially, wiping out their savings. They downsized to a smaller home and cut expenses where they could. But Karen had been a stay-at-home mom while raising their kids, and she had no marketable skills. They tried to juggle the bills, but bankruptcy hit them within a year.

They joined the ranks of the working poor. How could this happen, when Rick "felt great"?

The Lie

Like many men, Rick found it impossible to honestly accept his health problems, so he ignored any symptoms that might indicate a concern. He felt vulnerable and thought that if he acknowledged his feelings, things might get worse. He'd once heard that "ignorance is bliss," so he chose to love bliss and live in ignorance.

When he repeatedly said, "I feel great," he felt a little guilty, but he didn't stop saying it.

On the Receiving End

Karen knew her man and saw all the signs. She knew that Rick saw them, too, but wouldn't admit it. The resulting conflict impacted the core of their relationship. Karen felt shut out of Rick's inner life, and his health became one of those "danger zones" that just didn't get talked about, except with superficialities and denial.

She felt the gap widen each time she expressed her concern and he brushed it off. She did care about his health, but even more she cared about sharing their lives and talking about issues that touched them both. She had promised to love him "in sickness and in health," and she expected him to honestly face those sickness-and-health issues with her. When her expectation wasn't met, she felt ignored and that her husband devalued her opinions. He didn't seem to even consider what she knew she saw. His lack of consideration brought up a related issue of trust. If he didn't trust her enough to tell the truth about his health, what else was he hiding? In what other areas was he avoiding transparency?

Karen's anger grew, particularly after the first heart attack. She saw that Rick's denial put his life and their lifestyle at risk. When he got his first reality check and basically ignored it like he'd ignored her concerns, her frustration grew into resentment. She saw his attitude as a selfish deflection of genuine concern, and her perception colored other areas of their relationship.

Fear of being alone began to creep in. Karen genuinely loved Rick, and despite their inability to talk about this issue, she enjoyed their marriage. She feared that she might lose him. At this point, they'd spent a quarter of a century together and had webbed themselves together. She knew God would give the grace she needed, but she couldn't conceive how she'd manage without her life partner.

Fears of financial insecurity also plagued her. She felt guilty and embarrassed about those feelings, but she couldn't seem to avoid them. She was very aware of her lack of marketable skills, and she couldn't imagine having to fend for herself. If Rick died or became disabled, they'd be devastated financially. Putting their kids through college had drained their savings, and they'd planned on using the next twenty years to build their retirement. She'd gladly go to work, but what kind of wages would she get as a middle-aged woman with no experience or training? She hated the thought that his denial could put them in this spot.

And every time he said "I feel great" when he obviously didn't, these feelings and fears coursed through her.

Behind the Lie

As we mentioned in chapter 4, I (Tim) recently signed up for a flag-football league at our church. That will sound even more crazy when you realize that I played in the league two years before and badly tore my Achilles tendon in the second game. Before the tendon went, I broke a finger, straightened it out, and taped it up so I could return to the game. So why on earth did I run the risk of tearing the tendon again at the age of fifty-six?

The answer comes from a common masculine trait: stupidity. We men are stupid in that we truly do minimize physical problems. We minimize them because of a key part of our nature: reliance on physical strength and our ability to accomplish tasks.

MEN REJOICE IN STRENGTH

Strength may top the list when we examine the dimensions of masculinity. We're talking primarily about physical strength, but our discussion extends to personality, emotional, and vocal strength as well. Men like to perceive themselves as strong, and so they build that into their identity. That explains why I (Tim) played football again. I wanted to gauge how much physicality I had left in the tank! If my body had told me I didn't have anything left, I would have quit. Grudgingly, but I would have. But I just didn't want to give up on something physical unless I had to. And in our most recent game, I played defensive back against a teenager and gave up only one pass completion for about three yards. Women probably can't begin to understand how good that feels, but most guys could easily.

Let's explore a question: Did God design men this way? We think so. King David's last words reinforce this idea: "When the time drew near for David to die, he gave a charge to Solomon his son. 'I am about to go the way of all the earth,' he said. 'So *be strong, show yourself a man*" (1 Kings 2:1-2). David linked the manliness of his son to strength.

Solomon seemed to have gotten the message. He later wrote, "The glory of young men is their strength" (Prov. 20:29).

Men understandably capitalize on their strength when they are young. Young guys will wrestle one another for fun, but we've rarely seen women drag each other through the dirt for recreational purposes! A friend of Tim's got into the drywall business in his early twenties during one of the California building booms. He ran a lean business, wrote the bids, and did most of the work himself. He did well trading his physical strength for income.

As we mentioned earlier, men tend to build strength into their identity. They base much of their self-esteem on what they accomplish through their physical capabilities. That works pretty well until the strength starts to decline.

BUT STRENGTH DECLINES

Tim's friend the drywaller has now reached his fifties and finds it difficult to keep up with the physical aspect of his trade. He's now looking for a supervisory job. Why? He just can't physically do what he's done for the last thirty years. And although Tim still plays football, he doesn't play it like he did years ago. And he feels pain after every game!

The physical strength God puts within men when they're young doesn't continue, although men have a difficult time admitting to that. Just as God designed strength into men, the results of the Fall insure that strength won't last. A phrase in 2 Corinthians 4:16 makes this point clear: "Outwardly we are wasting away." We hit our physical peak in our twenties, then we head downhill. With each passing decade, our bodies experience significant change. We have to work harder to stay in shape. If we stop activity, we fall out of shape quickly. If we get injured, we take longer to recover.

Why? Our bodies experience aging and decay. They don't work like they used to. That's reality.

THE IMPACT ON MEN

Because physical strength plays such an important part of the masculine soul, men struggle to acknowledge its decline. Men can't easily admit to weakness and sickness because if they do, they lose part of their identity, what makes men "men." Not only do men lose much of their ability to do physical things as they age, but a major source of their self-esteem begins to disappear.

So men live in denial. When others mention a health problem they may possibly have, they shine it on. "I feel great physically." They don't feel great, but admitting it may be more difficult than actually facing the health issue.

Living the Truth

A wife needs to know how her husband's health affects his attitudes about himself and his marriage. The husband has a natural tendency to say he feels great even when he doesn't. So how can couples live in the truth? Let's look at three steps that can help.

ACCEPT REALITY

Our bodies decay. They lose strength. We will have health problems. Each of realities accelerates as we age, and death provides the only remedy. In communication classes students often hear the phrase "perception is reality." Our perceptions are reality, but they may not be accurate. Just because a husband may perceive that he feels great doesn't make his health great. But, he must deal with his perceptions realistically to live in the truth.

Husbands should have enough strength to handle the truth. Remember the line Jack Nicholson's character spoke in the movie *A Few Good Men?* "The truth? You want the truth? You can't *handle* the truth." Only real men have the strength to face the truth honestly and deal with it. And, truthfully, men's health problems increase with age. But that doesn't mean they lose their manhood. God provides an even better counterweight that we'll examine in the next section. But in the meantime, husbands do need to develop an accurate picture of their health. We encourage the men to read and ponder the following verses, which indicate that strength and health aren't the most important parts of life and that men can't always rely on them.

✢ "My heart pounds, my strength fails me; even
   the light has gone from my eyes" (Ps. 38:10).

✢ "This is what the Lord says:'Cursed is the one who trusts in man, who depends on flesh for his strength and whose heart turns away from the Lord'" (Jer. 17:5).

✢ "Outwardly we are wasting away" (2 Cor. 4:16).

✢ "The weakness of God is stronger than man's strength" (1 Cor. 1:25).

We have to begin with an attitude adjustment. Men need to realize and accept that aging and its decrepitude is the normal state of affairs.

THE BENEFITS OF AGING

If men only got older and more feeble, then aging would deeply devastate them. But God set up the process so that as the body wears out, men can grab onto more significant abilities than physical strength and health.

Greater Spiritual Maturity

Even as bodies wear out and succumb to the effects of aging, that very aging allows men to develop a closer connection with the spiritual realities. To help us make this connection, let's examine a familiar passage of Scripture. "Therefore we do not lose heart. Though *outwardly we are wasting away*, yet *inwardly we are being renewed* day by day. For our light and momentary troubles are achieving for us an eternal glory that far outweighs them all" (2 Cor. 4:16-17).

Men can easily get discouraged and lose heart when they can't do all they did before, all they built their identity on. But they can balance loss in the physical body with growth in the inner man, where we connect with God.

Developing a strong and stable relationship with God takes time. We sometimes experience the joy of a relationship that seems to click almost instantaneously, but it takes time to know whether the relationship will continue. To really know God, we have to go through good times and bad, joys and heartbreaks. We need to learn more about his nature, his heart, his revealed Word. That all takes time. So God balances physical decay with spiritual improvement. How foolish for anyone to substitute physical strength and health for the most important mark of success in life. "This is what the LORD says: 'Let not the wise man boast of his wisdom or the strong man boast of his strength or the rich man boast of his riches, but let him who boasts boast about this: that he understands and knows me'" (Jer. 9:23-24).

Rather than taking pride in their temporary physical strength, husbands can build their lives around the lasting trait of knowing God. Young men just can't know God as deeply as the old guys. Now, not all old guys know God deeply, perhaps because they've emphasized the physical world over the spiritual. But their age grants them the opportunity to focus on what lasts for eternity.

Greater Wisdom

A young intern interviewed the chief executive officer of a large company, one known for his practical insights. He asked about the source of his success.

"Very simple. Success comes from making wise decisions."

"Okay, but how did you learn to make wise decisions?"

"By making a lot of bad decisions."

Men, it takes time to make a lot of bad decisions! Maybe husbands can view aging as the opportunity to learn from a succession of bad decisions—made by them and others—so they can develop wisdom. Proverbs 20:29 gives this assurance: "The glory of young men is their strength, gray hair the splendor of the old."

Most husbands don't eagerly anticipate the onset of gray hair. Tim used to joke "better gray than gone," until both began to happen! He doesn't use that line anymore. God tells us that physical strength and health provide pride for young men, but that the older guys can take pride in advancing age because of the wisdom that can come with gray hair.

Tim's dad never went beyond the eighth grade in school, but he read widely and learned from what he experienced. Once

Tim got beyond his teen years when he thought he knew everything, he loved to get his dad's slant on things because his dad had a great deal of practical wisdom. No one has that kind of wisdom when he's young. It just takes time.

Older guys have that opportunity to grow in wisdom, even as their health diminishes.

Greater Reliance on God's Strength

In early years, many men try to accomplish spiritual tasks with their own energy and strength. Tim remembers a large number of ministry tasks that he thought he could accomplish if he only worked harder and smarter. He relied on the strength of his youth. It worked for a while. But over the years, two things occur.

First, that youthful strength decreases. The energy of the early years just doesn't exist like it did before.

Second, men discover that relying on that early energy doesn't work. Or, it doesn't work as much as relying on God's strength does. Several times, Tim tried to "force" spiritual issues and got battered. Since then, he's trying to let God set not only the agenda, but the pace as well. He's learning that God will work on the projects he most desires to see completed, and he will provide his touch at the right time.

The following verse shows how deeply God values our reliance on his strength: "This is what the LORD says: 'Cursed is the one who trusts in man, who depends on flesh for his strength and whose heart turns away from the LORD'" (Jer. 17:5). *Cursed!* That's a pretty strong word. Clearly, God doesn't want us to rely only on our own strength and not his. Yes, we should *use* our strength, but we can't *rely* on it as our primary source of spiritual success. Why? Another verse explains: "For the foolishness of God is wiser than man's wisdom, and *the weakness of God is stronger than man's strength*" (1 Cor. 1:25). If we need a sledgehammer to drive a stake into the ground and we have one available, why would we use a tack hammer? God provides much more strength than we have on our own.

The next verse tells men how to access the strength and wisdom of God: "The LORD will ... have compassion on his servants *when he sees their strength is gone*" (Deut. 32:36). As long as we have our strength and choose to rely on it, God will let us. But when we reach the end of our strength, then God will step in with his strength, his sledgehammer.

The passage seems to say that when husbands rely on their own strength and health, they have only limited resources. But acknowledging the insufficiency of their health and strength opens them up to experience the strength of God.

So, husbands, think about each twinge in your muscles, each gray hair, each sore spot, as a reminder that you can rely upon the spiritual strength of God in a greater manner. Once we accept the reality of aging and balance the disadvantages with the benefits, then we come to the third step in living in the truth.

CHERISH YOUR BODY

Face the decline. Live in the real world of imperfection, not on that river in Egypt called "de Nile." But don't give up. Many men observe their decreasing health and strength and decide to give up the battle. They don't exercise; they don't eat well, and as a result, they become even less physically able. We think that qualifies as sin. Why?

God gives us bodies to carry out his work on earth. The following selected verses from 1 Corinthians 6:13-20 have a dual meaning. The term *body* refers both to a person's physical body and to the church as the body of Christ. Paul applied the principle that God cares about our bodies to the area of sexual morality, but let's focus on the principle for our purposes.

> *The body is* not meant for sexual immorality, but *for the Lord*, and the Lord for the body. ... Do you not know that your bodies are members of Christ himself? Shall I then take the members of Christ and unite them with a prostitute? Never! Do you not know that he who unites himself with a prostitute is one with her in body? For it is said, "The two will become one flesh." But he

who unites himself with the Lord is one with him in spirit. Flee from sexual immorality. All other sins a man commits are outside his body, but he who sins sexually sins against his own body. Do you not know that your body is a temple of the Holy Spirit, who is in you, whom you have received from God? You are not your own; you were bought at a price. *Therefore honor God with your body.*

Our bodies provide a tool for God to use down here. A tool for us to give and receive pleasure, a tool to do things for others, and to do ministry for God. Without a body, we can't accomplish much of anything.

In a normal state, men care for their own bodies. So much, that in a passage we mentioned earlier, Paul encouraged men to give the same caliber of love to their wives as they give to their own bodies. "In this same way, husbands ought to love their wives *as their own bodies.* He who loves his wife loves himself. After all, no one ever hated his own body, but he feeds and cares for it, just as Christ does the church—for we are members of his body" (Eph. 5:28-30).

Husbands, feed and take care of your body. Be honest about your health—both to yourself and to your wife. Don't pretend to still be perfect. She knows you're not! And don't fear that if you mention your infirmities, you'll become a crying wimp, an always complaining hypochondriac. Avoid that extreme as much as you avoid the extreme of ignoring all physical complaints.

Get the checkups your doctor recommends. Listen to the concerns of your wife. Take the warning signs seriously. Some may not mean anything; some may indicate a serious problem you need to address. But address it, for the sake of your wife and the sake of ministry.

When you become honest about your physical health, you'll help your wife become more secure. She'll feel like she's a part of you. Take care of your body, and it will take care of you. But only when you face reality. And that's the truth.

Lie 7

I'm Not Lost; I Know Just Where We Are

The Truth about Asking for Help

The "Gal Pals" met for their monthly luncheon, and laughter, food, and gentle gossip filled their time.

"Hey girls, why did Moses wander for forty years in the wilderness?"

Silence.

"He wouldn't stop and ask for directions!"

Amber picked right up on the joke. "You wouldn't believe what happened to us last Saturday. We're driving to this wedding about fifty miles away, and my 'Moses' didn't take a map. Well, he took the wrong exit and we ended up on a dead-end street. It was awful! There was graffiti all over the buildings and trash strewn everywhere. We actually had to back out!

"We must have passed six gas stations before our rendezvous with terror, but would 'Daniel Boone,' fearless trailblazer, stop to get directions? Oh no! What did he say? 'I'm not lost; I know just where we are!' Yeah, right!

"We did get to the wedding before it started, but only because it started fifteen minutes late.

"Why are men like that? Why can't they just ask for help? Did God put some 'I don't need help' gene in all men? I just don't get it. They always try to seem so self-sufficient."

Vickie picked up where Amber left off. "I get so frustrated. You heard about Mike's heart attack two weeks ago, but let me give you the inside story. He spent some time paying bills in the study while I read in bed. Then about eleven, he comes in, gets his keys off the dresser, and says he has to go to the post office to mail a couple of bills that were almost late.

"He didn't go to the post office. He drove himself to the ER because he had these huge chest pains. He drove himself! Then, right on the table as they ran some tests, he had a major heart attack. Who did they call? Our pastor! Not me, but Pastor Wayne. He then came to the house and had to wake me up, since I'd fallen asleep. Then I had to get someone to watch Kylie and rush to the hospital. Why didn't he ask me? Why didn't he call 911? Why can't men ask for help?"

The Lie

Let's begin by looking at the first lie—"I'm not lost; I know just where we are." Men do tend to have a good sense of direction, and they usually aren't as lost as their wives think they are. But despite the friction in marriages that not asking for directions creates, this behavior masks a deeper lie: "I don't need any help. I can manage okay on my own."

Men struggle to ask for help of any kind. They want to appear strong, independent, and self-sufficient.

On the Receiving End

Both terror and anger filled Vickie as she drove to the hospital with Pastor Wayne that night. Fear of losing Mike; anger because he didn't tell her what was wrong. Then when she arrived, he instructed her to call some of his customers to tell them he wouldn't call on them for a few days. He still had to seem strong and in control.

Her first words to him? "If you do this again, you *better* die."

She did later forgive him, but his lying about his need influenced their relationship for some time.

Many husbands typically find it difficult to ask their wives for help. But what impact does their behavior have on their wives? The specific impact will vary based on the specific situation and the couple, but husbands need to be aware of some typical reactions.

ANGER

Vickie's anger represents a typical response. After all, Mike's show of independence put his life in jeopardy. He added unnecessary risks by driving to the hospital himself. Calling 911 would have provided medical attention fairly quickly, which is critical with heart problems. If his attack had come fifteen minutes earlier, he would have still been in the car. At least Vickie could have minimized the risk by driving him to the ER. She faced the prospect of a life without his presence, and much of the risk he took could have easily been avoided. His lack of consideration ticked her off, and understandably so.

RELATIONAL DISTANCE

Because God created husbands and wives to become one, when one doesn't rely on the other, the connection is diminished. The one feels unneeded, like she plays just a minor role in the other's life. Mike and Vickie had to work through these issues after he was released from the hospital.

Men have genuine needs for a life partner, which we'll explore later, but when they choose not to fully participate in sharing needs, they damage the marriage.

MISTRUST

Even now, several years later, Vickie warns Mike to "tell the truth, the whole truth, and nothing but the truth." Especially in the immediate aftermath, she feared that he might again hide significant issues from her. She made a logical connection: If he hid an oncoming heart attack, what else might he hide? Mike has crafted his own new life motto—"lies are heavy burdens; truth is easier to bear," and he regularly works toward being transparent in regard to his needs. He's learned he can ask for help without diminishing his masculinity and that God works better in the truth than in a lie.

Behind the Lie

Many men bask in the role of the rugged individual. Tim's dad typified this persona. Tremendously generous, he helped many of the neighbors in a variety of ways. Yet he rarely accepted any kind of help. He needed others to know he could provide for himself and his family; he could stand alone. Only in the last months of his life, as emphysema sapped his strength, did he finally allow others to help. At that point, however, he had little choice.

Why do men struggle so much with asking for help?

PRIDE

For many, pride tops the list. They value strength, as we discussed in the last lie. Power means "the ability to do," and men like doing. Accomplishments build their self-esteem. Accomplishments made while helping others build a sense of pride. Some men feel like they're better or stronger than those they help. And they don't want to appear needy because that's a sign of weakness. Needing help represents weakness; giving help represents strength.

SELF-SUFFICIENCY

Flowing from that trait of strength, many men feel that they possess all they need. They can meet the needs of their family; they can meet their own needs. Why show weakness and rely on others?

They compare fairly closely to the church in Laodicea: "You say, 'I am rich; I have acquired wealth and do not need a thing.' But you do not realize that you are wretched, pitiful, poor, blind and naked" (Rev. 3:17).

A self-sufficient attitude masks an underlying neediness that most husbands won't easily admit. So let's explore some truth about men, needs, and asking for help.

Living the Truth

Two basic principles might help husbands to understand and live in a greater level of truth.

MEN NEED HELP

Nearly every wife would instantly agree that men need help, and nearly every husband would resist it. But let's see what God says about men and their needs. God revealed the truth that men need help—particularly from their wives—back in the early days. In Genesis 2:18 (NLT), we read the familiar truth, "And the LORD God said, 'It is not good for the man to be alone. I will make a *companion* who will help him.'"

Other versions translate that word *companion* as *helper*, and some (wrongly) interpret that to mean that women should serve men. But a better meaning is "to rescue by providing strength that is lacking." Joshua 1:14–15 uses that word to describe army number one being a helper to army number two. Exodus 18:4 describes God himself as a "helper." The word doesn't imply weakness, but strength. So, because a man can't hack it alone, God provided a companion designed to help him.

Apart from God saying so, do men *really* need that help? Maggie Gallagher and Linda Waite researched the benefits of marriage in their book *The Case for Marriage*. Allow us to summarize ten benefits of marriage for men, in a David Letterman-like top-ten list.

10. *It's safer.* Bachelors experience violent crime four times more frequently than husbands.

9. *It can save your life.* Married men live ten years longer than single men.

8. *It can save your kid's life.* A parent's divorce decreases a child's life expectancy by four years.

7. *You earn more money.* After factoring in variables like college education and job history, husbands typically make 40 percent more than bachelors.

6. *You get richer.* The average married couple at retirement has assets of about $410,000, versus $167,000 for the never married and $154,000 for divorced men.

5. *You experience greater faithfulness.* Men who live with a woman cheat four times as often as husbands; women who live with a man cheat eight times more often than wives.

4. *It's healthier mentally.* Married men are less depressed, anxious, and distressed than single men.

3. *It makes you happier.* Forty percent of married people describe themselves as "very happy," while only 25 percent of singles do so.

2. *Your kids will love you more.* Adult children of divorce see both of their parents less and describe less positive relationships than when the parents remain married.

1. *Sex.* Married people have sex more frequently than singles and report more satisfying sex lives.

Ecclesiastes 4:9–12 gives more benefits of a good companion. Although the principles apply to companionship in general, they also apply to marriage.

> Two are better than one, because they have a good return for their work: If one falls down, his friend can help him up. But pity the man who falls and has no one to help him up! Also, if two lie down together, they will keep warm. But how can one keep warm alone? Though one may be overpowered, two can defend themselves. A cord of three strands is not quickly broken.

In marriage, our work brings more returns, and it benefits both people. We saw this in items 7 and 6 above. Marriage provides support in difficult times, yielding the results of 10, 9, 8, 4, 3, and 2. Marriage also provides intimacy, which we saw in items 5 and 1.

Clearly, men have genuine needs, and having many of those needs met by their wives is a great benefit of marriage. But in order for men to realize those benefits, they must take the next step.

Men Can Accept Help

Years ago, I (Tim) helped lead a mission trip to the small village of Penasco, outside Taos, New Mexico. The local contact told us they would arrange for us to rent a house for our group of nine to stay in for the month. Unfortunately, the day before our arrival the house deal fell apart, and we had no place to stay. One of the local leaders invited our group into her small home, and along with the six people in her family, we crammed a total of fifteen people into their house. We threw sleeping bags on the floor or slept outside; we ate assembly-line fashion and devastated their food budget. They wouldn't allow us to help out.

I felt terrible. We'd come to help them but ended up inconveniencing them greatly. I started to work out plans for us to purchase some camping gear and stay in a campground about fifteen miles away. Then John, my good friend and fellow leader, took me aside. "Tim, we need to give them a chance to express their love for us by meeting some of our needs. Helping has to go in both directions."

I'd been much too independent before and rarely allowed others to help me, which I'd learned from Dad. Mom and Dad helped with room and board my first year in college. After that, I paid for it all with scholarships and part-time jobs. I wanted to stand alone and not depend on others. In college, my attitude worked. In New Mexico, I was wrong, and John helped me see that.

Sheila and I have learned that we have needs that only others can fill and that we show great character when we ask for help. And God agrees. James gives just one example out of many about asking others: "Is any one of you sick? He should call the elders of the church to pray over him and anoint him with oil in the name of the Lord" (James 5:14). Restated, don't hesitate too much to ask for help from the appropriate source. Don't hesitate too much to accept help. We inserted the words *too much* on purpose. Knowing husbands, they *will* hesitate to ask for or accept help. You just can't change an innate trait instantly!

DEPEND ON OTHERS AND DEEPEN RELATIONSHIPS

Bob and Linda happened to sit at the same table at an alumni function. They'd vaguely known each other in college, but not well. They enjoyed their conversation, were intrigued with each other's life journey since college, and made plans to get together the next weekend. The relationship blossomed despite their living nearly 100 miles apart. But over time, Linda began to yearn for more connecting. The weekends didn't meet her needs for having enough time with a person she cared for.

And more significantly, Bob seemed remarkably self-contained. He enjoyed the level of their relationship, although he did his best to take her feelings into consideration. He made a sincere effort to meet her needs emotionally, conversationally, and spiritually—as much as he could, anyway. But he never revealed much about himself.

Linda couldn't quite put her finger on why the relationship didn't fully satisfy her. Until she met Roy at work. They began to talk, and she discovered the dimension that she missed with Bob. Roy needed her. Bob didn't. With Roy, her ability to meet his needs brought a deeper level to their friendship. And not much time passed before Bob had passed from the scene and Roy became her romantic interest.

Linda never knew that Bob had some deep needs within him and a desire to get closer to the right person. But he feared getting hurt, and he feared looking needy. So, in trying to protect himself, he lost a chance to have his needs met.

Husbands, learn from both Tim's dad and Bob. Tim grew closer to his dad than ever before during those months of being able to do something for his dad. He discovered that love needs to be expressed to grow to its maximum. Bob never gave himself a true chance with Linda because he wouldn't disclose his needs. He tried to appear self-sufficient and lost a promising relationship.

At the very core, love means doing something to benefit another. If husbands don't openly acknowledge their needs, then they deny their wives a chance to express love to them, which limits the depth of love they share. Husbands, you can acknowledge that you have needs. You can ask your wife to meet those needs. As you do, you'll see your marriage grow deeper. You'll see the partnership deepen. And that's the truth.

Lie 8

I Have to Work These Long Hours to Support the Family

The Truth about Working Too Much

Dana had made all the preparations for a great birthday party for Matt. All three kids had created their own birthday cards for Dad on the computer, with more than just a little help from Mom. She bought a new gas barbecue for him and had already set it up. He didn't have a clue about it. She had the tri-tip steaks ready.

The five of them would enjoy a nice meal cooked on the new grill, splurge on the fudge and chocolate cake, and then have a movie night at home. The kids had picked out a movie, one of their favorites. They *knew* Dad would enjoy it, too. He'd promised to be home by four to spend the time with the family.

At 4:15 the phone rang when she was outside, but Dana caught the message on the machine just after he hung up. "Hi, honey, I'm running a little over and didn't want you to worry. Doug asked me to fine-tune a proposal we're making tomorrow. I should have it done in half an hour. Be home soon. Looking forward to the party."

The frustration rose in Dana, but she pushed it down. She wouldn't let Doug ruin the night. But when Matt hadn't shown up by five, it swelled up again. She called him on his cell phone, hoping he'd left work. He hadn't. An edge crept into her voice.

"Okay, what is it now that's more important than being here with your family for your birthday party?"

"I can't help it. I really can't. Doug and I found some flaws in the figures on the proposal. If we present it tomorrow the way it is now, we'd kill the deal. We have to crunch some numbers and plug in the new results. It won't take much longer. Can you give me forty-five minutes to finish this off?"

"Do I have a choice?"

Dana hung up and turned to face little Jeff. "Where's Daddy? We need him for his birthday party! I like parties."

Seven-year-old Ryan chipped in, "I'm hungry. Can we eat before Daddy gets home? He's late a lot."

Dana fired up the barbecue, cooked the meal, and the four of them laughed a lot as they ate. Just as she put the dishes in the dishwasher, the front door opened.

"Daddy! You're home!" The kids rushed Matt, competed to hug him, and wished him a happy birthday. "Now we can watch the movie!"

Matt fixed a plate of cold food and they all gathered in the family room to watch the movie. Dana didn't say much. Not then. She waited until they ate their cake, gave Matt his presents, and put the kids to bed.

"Matt, how could you do this again? The kids counted on your party so much. They even helped get the food together; they talked about giving you a good party all day. But you cared less for them than you do that project at work. This happens *way* too often."

"You know, Dana, you don't seem to mind living in this nice house. And you seem to enjoy your Explorer, too. Yeah, I work overtime a lot. The company pretty much demands it. And I know you wish I could spend more time at home. But I have to work these long hours to support the family. Without that, we'd be on the streets. Do you want that?"

The Lie

Matt did work long hours. He did support the family. But deeper than supporting the family, Matt worked so much to shore up his self-esteem. He felt worthwhile while working. And, in his quiet moments, he knew he liked all the material stuff that the long hours provided. He *said* he did it for the family, but he knew better. Mostly, he did it for himself.

On the Receiving End

Dana continued. "Matt, I married you to *be* married to you. I made a decent living before we got married. Not like you do now, but I did well. I didn't need to have someone support me financially. I want *you*. You as a person. Your time. Your interest when you're here.

"We have a lot of nice things. I enjoy them, but I need you. I want us to share our lives. But when you put in so many hours, the kids and I just get the leftovers. When you come home, you eat dinner—often after we have—then you drop in front of the TV, play a little with the kids, read them a story, and crash. The next day, it starts all over again. You don't know how much you disappointed the kids when you were late for your own birthday party. They worked so hard.

"I've kept track; you've worked six out of the last eight Saturdays. And most days you put in at least ten hours. That doesn't leave much time for us. I appreciate how hard you work, I really do. But I don't think you put in those hours for us. Not completely. You do it a lot for yourself. I don't know why, but you do."

Like many women with husbands who work too much, Dana felt shut out of Matt's life. She sometimes wondered if he merely wanted a bed partner, housekeeper, and someone to raise the kids. She certainly didn't feel like a life partner, more like a business partner. At least she didn't worry about unfaithfulness with him; he didn't have enough time.

Behind the Lie

Two primary traits afflict the masculine gender; each makes men more susceptible to investing too much time in work at the expense of their families.

THE NEED TO DO

For some time, feminists proclaimed that males and females differed because we were taught to act differently. Boys played with trucks because we gave them trucks; girls played with dolls because we gave them dolls. Research contradicts that theory. We heard Dr. James Dobson on his radio show, *Focus on the Family*, mention a fascinating study. Researchers handed crib babies a toy. At this stage, we haven't taught them much about gender roles. Almost without exception, boy babies reached for the toy. Almost without exception, girl babies reached for the hand holding the toy.

Most researchers agree that men tend to get their self-worth from their accomplishments, primarily their work. Women tend to get their self-worth from their relationships, primarily their marriages.

God designed those differences into the genders. Back in Genesis, just after Adam and Eve allowed sin into the world, God announced the consequences. Adam faced the consequences of work becoming more difficult.

> To Adam he said, "Because you listened to your wife and ate from the tree about which I commanded you, 'You must not eat of it,' Cursed is the ground because of you; through painful toil you will eat of it all the days of your life. It will produce thorns and thistles for you, and you will eat the plants of the field. By the sweat of your brow you will eat your food until you return to the ground, since from it you were taken; for dust you are and to dust you will return." (Gen. 3:17–19)

Eve faced the consequences of her marriage becoming more difficult. "I will greatly increase your pains in childbearing; with pain you will give birth to children. Your desire will be for your husband, and he will rule over you" (Gen. 3:16).

For both men and women, our natural tendencies became our greatest area of vulnerability. Men particularly slip into a problem when they emphasize work and try to do too much. God originally assigned work to Adam: "The LORD God took the man and put him in the Garden of Eden to *work it and take care of it*" (Gen. 2:15). But sin tweaks the innate tendency of men to gain satisfaction from their work into work dominating their lives. Matt experienced that, and Dana felt the consequences in her marriage.

THE LOVE OF STUFF

Years ago, a popular bumper sticker read, "The only difference between men and boys is the cost of their toys." Because men like doing, they need stuff to do it with. So men love their dirt bikes, fishing gear, boats, ski equipment, athletic gear, and trucks and cars. We suspect that before too long, researchers will find a "stuff" gene in the male DNA.

Often we forget that stuff comes from God! God gave us stuff to enjoy life and our physicality. Psalm 104 praises God for the good things he has done: "He makes grass grow for the cattle, and plants for man to cultivate—bringing forth food from the earth: wine that gladdens the heart of man, oil to make his face shine, and bread that sustains his heart" (vv. 14-15).

To Jewish people, having a lot of children and living a long time marked a successful life. God gave a different opinion: "A man may beget a hundred children, and live many years; but however many are the days of his years, if he does not *enjoy life's good things*, or has no burial, I say that a stillborn child is better off than he" (Eccl. 6:3 NRSV).

God wants us to enjoy the stuff of life! Unfortunately, men can go overboard here if they think that stuff demonstrates a successful life. Jesus taught otherwise. "Beware! Don't be greedy for what you don't have. Real life is not measured by how much we own … a person is a fool to store up earthly wealth but not have a rich relationship with God" (Luke 12:15, 21 NLT).

Matt enjoyed his house and yard, his nice car, and the toys he could use on occasion. Like many men, he fell into the deception of stuff. He ignored more important issues to have nice things.

Living the Truth

Based on these two vulnerabilities—the need to do and loving stuff—we suggest that men develop a strategy to address them directly. When husbands develop a biblical understanding of the issues, then they can live more fully in the truth.

BUILD BIBLICAL SELF-WORTH

Husbands can counter their innate tendency to build self-worth on achievement and activity. For guys, work will always play a role in making up their identity, but they can move it out of a primary and into a contributing role. In movie terms, let your work win an Oscar as best supporting actor, not as best lead actor.

Allow us to suggest three sources of self-worth. Incidentally, the first two apply fully to women as well, and the third can be adapted.

A Matchless Identity

Many men want to know they stand out from the crowd. Few men yearn to be just another "man in a gray flannel suit." Typically, they use the amount and quality of their work to achieve the distinction they crave. But not everyone can stand out, only those with exceptional talent or drive. Some never get enough success; others get too much. Does that put the average guy in a bind if he can't reach his goal? Yes, if he only uses work as the means to achieve it. God provides an alternative, one available to all men.

We've all been amazed at the revelations about DNA, how saliva left on a water glass can give a solid identification. But DNA provides just one dimension of uniqueness. Fingerprints, retinal patterns, blood typing, facial dimensions, and the sound of a voice all work together to make each individual "one of a kind."

But God gives another unique trait to men who love Jesus: a unique position in his church. In 1 Corinthians 12:7–31, Paul used the human body as a metaphor for the church as the body of Christ. He taught that every Christian is a member of the body and that the Holy Spirit gives us spiritual gifts. He taught that each person is unique, that all members possess equal value. He taught that God connects every member into one body and that the body needs every member, regardless of how important or unimportant they may seem to some.

In a previous book, I used Rick Warren's **SHAPE** concept. Rick teaches that each Christian has a unique makeup. He uses **SHAPE** as an acronym for **S**piritual gift, **H**eart, **A**bilities, **P**ersonality, and **E**xperience. No one else can come close to combining our spiritual gifts, what we get excited about, our natural abilities, our individual personality, and our life experiences. These qualities make us into a totally unique individual that God designed.

Husbands can begin to build a godly self-image from realizing that no one else can match them. They may not stand out in a crowd, but no one can duplicate exactly who they are.

A Matchless Value

Too often, men build their self-worth based on a comparison to others. As long as they come out better than someone else, then they have value. Or they build their worth on achievement. After all, that's what their employers do. High producers get rewarded. Low producers get fired. In the major leagues, .300 hitters have more value to the team than players who hit .220. The .300 hitter gets paid several million to play a boy's game. The .220 hitter applies for unemployment. Based on their experience, men accept these methods to build their self-esteem.

God has a different perspective on the value of a person. First, he created every human in his own likeness.

> Then God said, "Let us make man *in our image,* in our likeness, and *let them rule* over the fish of the sea and the birds of the air, over the livestock, over all the earth, and over all the creatures that move along the ground."

> So God created man in his own image, in the
> image of God he created him; male and female
> he created them. (Gen. 1:26–27)

Flowing from that image, God gave man the responsibility of wisely ruling over the earth. These two factors—image and ruling—both speak to an innate value in people, including husbands. God doesn't link this value to achievement or comparison, but to creation and identity.

Second, every man possesses an innate link to the spiritual dimension. Let's stay in Genesis. "The LORD God formed the man from the dust of the ground and breathed into his nostrils the breath of life, and the man became a living being" (2:7).

The actual life of each man comes from God giving his spirit. That spirit within each man provides the incalculable value of having the ability to connect with God. With this information, men can build self-worth based on both their creation in God's image and from God's breath giving them life.

Third, men can build their self-worth based on their cost. Some time ago, we had a used Volvo to sell, so we checked out the classified ads and the Kelly Blue Book to determine its value. We put those figures together, factored in the condition of the car, and came up with a selling price. But not everyone who looked at the car thought it had the same value we did. We discovered its true value was what some real person would pay for it. Not what Kelly told us, not what we thought, but what a person would give in exchange.

Read this next verse to see the value God places on every man who's ever lived. "For God so loved the world that he gave his one and only Son, that whoever believes in him shall not perish but have eternal life" (John 3:16). God loved people so much that he paid his Son. You might want to insert your name in place of "the world." That gives a better picture. Men have a matchless identity and value with which to create the foundation of their self-worth. Once they have that unshakeable base, then, and only then, can they move to the next step. Here comes the Oscar for best supporting role.

Honest Self-appraisal

Read the two following passages, and then we'll pull out several factors that help husbands build a godly self-worth, one that doesn't rely primarily on achievement or comparison.

> For by the grace given me I say to every one of you: Do not think of yourself more highly than you ought, but rather think of yourself with sober judgment, in accordance with the measure of faith God has given you. (Rom. 12:3)

> If anyone thinks he is something when he is nothing, he deceives himself. Each one should test his own actions. Then he can take pride in himself, without comparing himself to somebody else, for each one should carry his own load. (Gal. 6:3-5)

First, we're not to think too highly of ourselves (Rom. 12:3; Gal. 6:3). We're not to think we have more value than anyone else. Why? God created each person with the same value, in his image and with his spirit. We may be better than some others in some things, but our innate value remains constant.

Second, we're to think of ourselves as we "ought" (Rom. 12:3). But how "ought" we to think of ourselves? We need to view ourselves as people of value, as we've seen. We need to view ourselves as unique individuals. We need to view ourselves with love. Remember Ephesians 5:28-29? "Husbands ought to love their wives as their own bodies. He who loves his wife loves himself. After all, no one ever hated his own body, but he feeds and cares for it." We normally love ourselves. We ought not to think of ourselves as more or less valuable than anyone else. We're all different, but we all have equal value.

Third, we test our own actions (Eph. 6:4), according to faith (Rom. 12:3) and not in comparison to others. Rather, we need to ask ourselves, Are we making progress in becoming more like Christ? Do we strive to follow God's standards—not our own or those of the world? When we can answer yes—even occasionally—our accomplishments, especially spiritual ones, contribute to godly self-esteem.

Of course, all that we do—on the job, at home, and on the road—should flow from our faith, according to Romans 14:23: "Everything that does not come from faith is sin." Our faith should impact how we work, how we treat people, even how we mow our lawns! When we see that our faith is permeating our actions, we can move toward the result, which comes next.

Fourth, we can take pride in our lives (Eph. 6:4). All of these facets of self-appraisal combine to create a tapestry of self-worth. Not self-worth built on accomplishment on the job. Not self-worth built on comparisons to others. But a self-worth based on how God created us with value and spirit and what we do with our lives spiritually. As husbands create a godly self-image, they can fight the demon of workaholism, but winning the battle requires another dimension of strategy.

VIEW STUFF AS A TOOL, NOT A GOAL

Too many men give their lives to the pursuit of stuff they can't take with them and that innately *cannot satisfy the deepest needs of life.* Yet they invest their time, energy, and talents in a vain attempt to grab onto what they cannot hold. Hebrews 13:5 states this concept clearly: "Keep your lives free from the love of money and be content with what you have, because God has said,'Never will I leave you; never will I forsake you.'"

Everything else being equal—which never happens, of course—most of us would rather have money and stuff than not have it. But Hebrews tells us not to want it too much and to counter our desire to acquire with contentment. How can we do that? By realizing that what we already have—God—has more value than stuff and will remain with us for eternity.

Yet do we invest our lives in crafting our connection to God or to getting more stuff? Husbands, think carefully about this. Your innate inclination to work can easily seduce you away from God the Creator toward God's created things.

Proverbs 23:4 gives some good advice for husbands who struggle with too many hours on the job. "Do not wear yourself out to get rich; have the wisdom to show restraint." God gave work to men as a privilege and a responsibility. But exercise enough wisdom to restrain yourself from giving your life to the pursuit of the material stuff of life at the expense of your relationships with God and your wife. Exert some self-control.

Examine how your genuine needs differ from your wants. Work hard for the needs. Show restraint on the wants. Leave enough time in your lives for your wife, your kids, your leisure. Or change how you view stuff.

Look on stuff as a lousy goal, but a great tool. As a goal, it wears out. You can't take all that stuff to heaven, and using it doesn't really satisfy. Most often it merely increases our hunger for more. But it works marvelously at two tasks: It helps us to enjoy life and it helps us minister to others. This next passage expresses these two dimensions.

> Remember this: Whoever sows sparingly will also reap sparingly, and whoever sows generously will also reap generously. Each man should give what he has decided in his heart to give, not reluctantly or under compulsion, for God loves a cheerful giver. And God is able to make all grace abound to you, so that in all things at all times, *having all that you need*, you will *abound in every good work*. As it is written: "He has scattered abroad his gifts to the poor; his righteousness endures forever." Now he who supplies seed to the sower and bread for food will also supply and increase your store of seed and will enlarge the harvest of your righteousness. You will be made rich in every way so that you can be generous on every occasion, and through us your generosity will result in thanksgiving to God. (2 Cor. 9:6–11)

We can use the stuff of life both for meeting our needs and for blessing others. Particularly, we put our families first. Working and making a living are a powerful tool to take care of our families. We don't have families to take care of us so we can work, as Matt believed.

PRACTICAL SUGGESTIONS

Keith began working as a box boy at a major supermarket chain in southern California while still in high school. He worked both smart and hard, progressed to checker while going to college, and then to managing the produce department. Along the way, he married Gloria, a co-worker, and two kids soon became part of the family.

Not long after, he became the store's assistant manager, and the executives had their eye on him as managerial material. He'd barely entered his thirties when they gave him his own store, an older rundown one, but his own. He incorporated some of the changes he'd learned in his MBA program and the store thrived. Upper management next moved him to a larger, brand-new store, and Keith knew he'd arrived.

By then the family had started going to church; Gloria thought they should with the kids. Keith began to grapple with concepts of spiritual priorities and families, and soon he discovered that much of what he'd been doing presented a conflict. Then the company sent all managers to a teamwork-building conference, and Keith heard them encourage the managers to put their families first, to work hard but not to sacrifice family for career.

He liked what he heard, and so did Gloria when he came back. They started talking about how they would put their family first. Things would have to change; they both recognized that.

Once again, though, the company started requiring more time from Keith, despite the good things said at the conference. Keith felt the pull of conflicting messages. He talked to his supervisors; they didn't see a change coming to lighten the load. So he and Gloria talked and prayed about it at length, and then he resigned to pursue a career in mortgage loans. He was sure his new career wouldn't require the time at work that his old job had; he could spend more time with the family. They had to sacrifice financially, but both Keith and Gloria thought they made a good call.

This couple typifies the two steps we recommend for reprioritizing. First, sit down with your wife and clearly and frankly talk about your concerns and needs. Determine how you can best balance work and family. Try to establish some hard parameters of what is and isn't acceptable, along with some flexible parameters.

Second, evaluate the options—the benefits and costs of each—and make some hard decisions. Some careers, as Keith discovered, don't allow enough flexibility for time with your family. Decide what you want the most, based upon what's most important. Factor in the priorities we've talked about in this chapter. You may choose to make a job change if the flexibility isn't there. For some, like Matt, the job has the flexibility; he just puts in extra hours on his own.

After twenty-five years in ministry, Tim has now done over eighty-five funerals. Not once does he recall an employer giving a eulogy that praised the deceased for sacrificing family time to serve the company.

Husbands, honestly look at yourselves to see if you've been prone to working long hours and telling your family it's for them. Build a solid sense of self-esteem, and develop a biblical perspective on stuff. Then, spend time with your family. They'll appreciate it. And that's the truth.

Lie 9

I'm Sorry; I Won't Do That Again

The Truth about Repentance

Mimi reached down to pick up Gerardo's dirty socks from the closet floor. Again.

She found them just a foot or so from the dirty clothes hamper. When she saw him walk into the bedroom, she couldn't help herself.

"Honey, I've asked you a million times. Can you *please* not leave your dirty clothes all over the bedroom and bathroom? It would save me a lot of work if you'd just put them in the hamper. I know you can throw them in. I've seen you make longer shots at church basketball games!"

"Baby, I'm sorry. I guess I got distracted. I know it's important to you, and I won't do it again. Promise!"

A few weeks later, she kissed him good-bye as he headed for work and she moved into the kitchen. The recycling can was so full it almost spilled over onto the floor. She knew she had a lot more stuff to go into it, too, and there simply was no room. So she womanhandled it out to the larger recycling container and strained to empty the can. Because of its weight, she couldn't quite handle it, and a lot of the stuff spilled onto the sidewalk. Frustrated, she picked it all up and went on with her day.

Gerardo found the refilled can at the front door when he arrived home that night. He took the not-so-subtle hint, emptied the can, and walked in. "I'm so sorry, honey. I didn't notice the can was full. I'll try to do better."

"Gerardo, that's the second time today it's been emptied. You left the house with it full, and I made a mess trying to get it into the big one. You know I'm not strong enough to empty it. I really need some help here."

"I know. My mind was on work today, and I never noticed it. Sorry."

Not too long after, they met with their small group, and the conversation turned to Emeril's show on the Food Channel. Gerardo couldn't resist. "Gang, nobody's wife cooks quite like mine. I mean, she uses the smoke alarm as a cooking timer! Good thing we have long-life batteries in it!"

Mimi had a few words for him on the way home. "Gerardo, how often have I asked you to not make fun of my cooking with the group? I do the best I can. Some of those women are awesome cooks, and you make me sound like a junior high girl in home economics class. I feel belittled when you do that."

"Mimi, I really am sorry. It just popped out of my mouth. I didn't think. I won't do it again. Honest."

The Lie

Many husbands discover that saying "I'm sorry; I won't do that again" seems to cover a multitude of sins. The words get them off the hook for their wrongs, and they can avoid dealing with the real issues. In truth, they don't feel that much sorrow, because they continue their behavior. They don't particularly intend to stop what they're doing; they just want to stop talking about it.

On the Receiving End

Mimi felt frustrated as Gerardo continued to evade dealing with the issues she brought up. When he insincerely told her what she wanted to hear, her irritation increased. She found it hard to get deeper into the issues when he agreed on the surface. After each encounter, she felt like they'd missed getting to the heart of things, but she didn't know how to get to where she knew they needed to go.

As the pattern continued, she saw him and his "I'm sorry; I won't do that again" as the boy who cried wolf. She just couldn't believe him.

Her frustration began to brew into anger and resentment. She felt shut out of Gerardo's life when he regularly avoided conflict. Nothing got resolved or even discussed. Mimi's anger bled over into other areas of the relationship because, though her husband didn't seem aware of it, he was eroding trust and communicating a lack of care for his wife.

One day, while talking to a friend, she summarized it. "I think he just wants to avoid conflict. He thinks that if he gives his old line, I'll just shut up and believe him. But things don't change; we repeat the same stuff over and over. I feel like there's a cancer in our marriage, and he wants to just put a Band-Aid on it. Someday, he's going to have to deal with these issues."

Behind the Lie

Gerardo's patterns typify the behavior of many husbands. They think saying "I'm sorry" will work as a cure-all for every relationship problem. Just say those two magic words and immediately everything is fine again, right? Well, no, but why do husbands rely on those two words so much? Three primary tendencies lead men into that lie.

AVOIDANCE OF CONFLICT

Men typically like to live in harmony. They may battle in the workplace, but they long for peace and tranquility at home, and family provides a refuge from the strife and stress in the outside world. Because of this desire, they develop a strategy that often works—for a while. To insure domestic tranquility, they draw back from engaging in conflict or from anything that may even look like an overt disagreement.

Saying "I'm sorry" often calms the stormy seas of conflict. The husband doesn't disagree with his wife, and he doesn't get defensive. He just deflects the issue. He gives in a little with the apology; he recognizes that his wife has a valid point. He gives in a little with the promise to not do it again; he recognizes he should have acted differently. He may even appease her and do the job for a couple of weeks until she forgets about it.

On the surface, then, the issue appears resolved. But the phrase was a sham. Rather than resolution, the husband sought only deflection. He doesn't want to deal with a big disagreement, so he acknowledges the accuracy of his wife's comments. But he never intends to change. He just wants to keep things on an even keel and avoid overt conflict.

Too often, husbands baptize their desire for harmony and peace. They read verses like Proverbs 17:14: "Starting a quarrel is like breaching a dam; so drop the matter before a dispute breaks out." They make sure the matter gets dropped before it becomes a dispute, and they believe they've acted as a spiritual leader and avoided a needless quarrel.

Or they read Proverbs 20:3 and rejoice in their honorable actions: "It is to a man's honor to avoid strife, but every fool is quick to quarrel." So they say, "I'm sorry; I won't do that again." And as they do, they rejoice in their wisdom in averting the foolishness of a quarrel. Are the wives rolling their eyes yet?

Avoidance of Confession

Some men find it especially difficult to ever admit they're wrong. Author Andrew Greeley used a phrase to describe one man, though it probably applies to many: "Seldom wrong, but never in doubt." Perhaps this attitude comes from the masculine need to appear strong, which includes refusing to acknowledge failure. Admitting to mistakes or failures not only hurts the masculine self-image, it also calls into question a husband's ability to serve as a spiritual leader, doesn't it?

Gerardo grew up in a critical family and soon discovered that when you admitted a mistake, they never let you forget it. If you denied it, then you could at least continue to defend yourself. But once you admitted it, they knew they were right.

Many men have experiences similar to Gerardo's, so to avoid a full admission, they give a grudging and partial confession: "I'm sorry." Enough to avoid the fullness of truth and having to deal with those consequences, but not an outright lie.

In truth, they may only be sorry that their wives caught them. They may only be sorry that it bothered them. But their words divert attention enough so that the husbands can avoid getting to the heart of the issue.

AVOIDANCE OF CHANGE

If the husband admits he made a mistake, then the admission carries some moral obligation to change his behavior. Many men have no desire to change, so they won't acknowledge that what they did was truly wrong.

Gerardo loved having a good time and laughing. He frequently played the role of the jokester to keep a gathering loose. And what better target for humor did he have than his wife? He didn't mind appeasing her sensitivity on the issue of her cooking as long as he could make a joke every so often to liven up the group. He said he was sorry, but he really had no intention of stopping the comments about her cooking. The payoffs were far more important than the consequences.

All three of these masculine traits—avoidance of conflict, confession, and change—combine to make it difficult for many husbands to transcend the lie "I'm sorry; I won't do that again."

Living the Truth

For husbands to get beyond the lie and to live in the truth, we must address each of the reasons that make men susceptible to this lie. Let's look at the solution to each tendency.

EMBRACE CONFLICT

Husbands will begin to journey toward truth when they realize that every marriage will have conflict. Science defines friction as two uneven surfaces that rub against one another and thereby produce heat. That sounds like marriage, doesn't it? Both husbands and wives are imperfect and have rough edges. The more they interact, or the more they rub on each other, the more heat gets produced. But how can we bring tranquility out of chaos?

Romans 12:16 gives us a simple command: "Live in harmony with one another." Most husbands yearn for that and avoid any form of conflict. But that strategy merely pushes the issue below the surface and doesn't resolve the disagreement.

For a very short time, Tim played the guitar with several friends. But he could never tune the guitar; his ear just couldn't pick up the different sounds. So he'd tune it the best he could and begin playing, until the other players couldn't ignore the discord. Even though Tim didn't hear a problem—or wouldn't acknowledge it—the problem still existed. When it became unbearable, one of the guys would take the guitar, tune it properly, and they'd go on and try to make musical harmony.

Husbands need to realize that recognizing and dealing with disharmony offers the marriage what tuning offered Tim's band: genuine harmony. Trust us, you don't want your marriage to sound like Tim's guitar playing!

By encouraging husbands to embrace conflict, we don't ask them to start fights for no reason at all. Rather, they need to recognize that an issue exists. Embracing reality means acknowledging the conflict. Only then can true harmony develop.

Conflict can cover a wide range of issues. Some of them deal with personal preferences, like doing the laundry. Some issues deal with moral wrong, like husbands insulting their wives in public. But when one partner sees something as an issue, it becomes an issue for both of them, and it needs genuine resolution.

Husbands, if you sometimes use the deflection of saying you're sorry, we encourage you to make an attitude adjustment. View unresolved issues as decreasing the harmony you desire. Without resolution, your wife's feelings of anger, resentment, and frustration will continue to build. Like a bent hose that's rapidly filling with water, you'll find her exploding over future issues— issues that could have been minimized if you had faced them together from the beginning.

Think of resolution as giving a little to gain a lot. You do give up some surface harmony now as you deal with the conflict, and dealing with issues *will* definitely increase temporary difficulties. This is where you do the giving. When you deal with the conflict right away, you increase the long-term harmony of the relationship. Why? Because you've recognized and worked on your wife's concerns. You stop the process of emotions building until they spill over. And that's where you gain—a lot!

Resolution doesn't mean that you both must agree. Rather, you bring the issue out into the open and work through it with the following two strategies.

EMBRACE CONFESSION

Embracing confession allows husbands to live in truth. *Confession* merely means "to say the same thing." Not that you say the same thing as your wife, but that what you say matches reality. You say what God would say. Acknowledge the truth—the full truth—about the event to yourself. Admit that truth to God. And admit that truth to your wife. Not only is confession good for your marriage, it's biblical. "Therefore each of you must put off falsehood and *speak truthfully* to his neighbor, for we are all *members of one body*" (Eph. 4:25).

In this verse, Paul talked to people in the church. They needed to speak truthfully because they all composed the body of Christ. If Sheila cuts her thumb, it impacts the functioning of her entire body. Speaking truthfully to one another has an effect on both parties, and this principle applies even more to husbands and wives, who are connected so very intimately in one body.

When husbands lie by saying they're sorry and won't do it again even though they fully intend to do it again, they violate the concept of the body. This means that if husbands did something wrong, they must admit that it was wrong. Otherwise, the body—the marriage—will not function as God intended.

I (Tim) have discovered the tremendous freedom that comes from admitting rather than excusing wrongs. As a side benefit, it disarms the wife. When a husband avoids the generic

"I'm sorry" and says, "I was wrong. I forgot. Will you forgive me?" he defuses his wife's time bomb of anger and frustration. Couples don't have to argue about whether something happened. Instead they can focus on how to act better in the future.

Mimi said to her friend, "I wouldn't mind what he did if he'd just admit it. But when he denies it or tries to slide past it, it becomes bigger than the original issue."

EMBRACE CHANGE

Embracing conflict and confession will allow the third step: making concrete changes where needed. If the issue represents a moral wrong, then husbands should desire God's best in their lives more than they desire to continue in the old behavior. If the issue represents making life easier for their wives, then husbands must choose to value expressing love by how they act.

Love means action. John 3:16 links them clearly: "For God so *loved* the world that he *gave* his one and only Son, that whoever believes in him shall not perish but have eternal life."

Romans 5:8 echoes the connection: "But *God demonstrates his own love* for us in this: While we were still sinners, *Christ died for us.*"

In both verses, God acted in the best interests of those he loves. Husbands, does deflecting conflict in an area that bothers your wife demonstrate love for her? Why would you want to increase stress and difficulty for the person you love?

We're now at the very heart of the entire issue. Husbands, we're not trying to tell you to give in to every whim of your wives. Doing so doesn't necessarily benefit them. But committing yourself to act in ways that make life easier for your wife will go a long way toward creating the harmony you desire so much.

Perhaps what you've done is morally wrong. Then stop it. Perhaps what you've done is a personal preference, a conflict where neither choice is necessarily the "right" one. Can you compromise? Either way, don't shy away from the conflict that comes when you deal with the issue in a frank manner. And don't shy away from acknowledging the truth.

What seems to bother wives the most is when their husbands think words by themselves are enough. Most would prefer a husband to say that he will continue doing what he wants to rather than to say he will stop when he has no intention of doing so. Jesus agreed.

"What do you think? There was a man who had two sons. He went to the first and said, 'Son, go and work today in the vineyard.'

"'I will not,' he answered, but later he changed his mind and went.

"Then the father went to the other son and said the same thing. He answered, 'I will, sir,' but he did not go.

"Which of the two did what his father wanted?" (Matt. 21:28-31)

What counts the most with God and with most wives? Doing the right thing. Not using words to deflect conflict, to avoid changing your behavior. Words mean very little without behavior that lives them out. Husbands, if you say you're sorry and keep on doing what offends your wife, you don't live in the truth. But when you say, "I was wrong; I won't do it again," and you don't do it again, then you'll discover that you have an entirely new wife. And that's the truth.

Lie 10

I Know Just What You Need to Do

The Truth about Advice and Support

In the early days of our marriage, we both worked at full-time jobs: Sheila in the purchasing division of a pharmaceutical company, and Tim as an associate pastor overseeing all of the youth ministry at our church. He also worked directly with the college/career group where Sheila worked as an adult sponsor. Job and church responsibilities consumed several nights each week, some Saturdays, and most of Sundays.

Each evening after getting off work, we'd sit on the couch with soft drinks in our hands and debrief, sharing the events of our days. We cherished that time to reconnect each day. Sheila's job brought a lot of frustrations, though, and one time she talked about something that happened at work.

"I know just what you need to do," Tim replied, and he proceeded to detail a clear strategy on how she could deal with the situation. In a typical masculine manner, he felt proud that he could help his wife deal with her struggles at work.

Several weeks later, the big problem focused on dealing with a supplier who gave inconsistent service. Again, with a manly fix-it attitude, Tim made some suggestions that he thought might help. "I had to deal with something like that at my last job. You might try ..." Once again, he felt good about supporting his wife.

The next time she shared a work concern, he again began, "I know what you can do. Try ..."

That's all he got out before Sheila interrupted. "Hold on, Tim. I know you mean well, but I'm not a dummy. I've been there for twelve years now, and I've gotten some nice promotions and raises. I'm good at what I do. I *know* the steps to take. I just need someone to listen to me, someone who'll care, who'll take my side. I don't need advice."

The Lie

Like many men, Tim's task orientation made him quick to offer advice on how to fix a problem. Men tend to do well at analyzing situations and crafting a strategy to address them. But his underlying attitude—"I know just what you need to do"—represents a lie, because wives don't need a solution. They need emotional support. Husbands *don't* know just what their wives need, and because of their lack of knowledge, they provide the wrong thing.

On the Receiving End

When Tim tried to "fix" the problems for her, Sheila felt just a bit demeaned, like he thought she couldn't figure it out herself. She felt that Tim had a condescending attitude, that he thought he was smarter than she. She never thought that sharing her difficulties at work meant that she was asking for advice.

So what did she want? What did she desire when she talked about her struggles? She wanted a companion, someone to sit beside her and understand. As demonstrated in this illustration, Sheila's desire for a companion touched three basic areas.

First, she wanted *comfort*. The encounters at work left her uneasy, a little discouraged. She needed an arm around her, the presence of a special person who cared for her. Her heart cried out for unconditional love and acceptance that would provide strength through the stress. She needed someone next to her, like the Holy Spirit, the Comforter, who comes alongside us.

Second, she wanted *support*. Not support in figuring out what to do, but support from someone who would keep her from falling into the pit of despondency. She wanted a safety net of care.

Third, she wanted *understanding*. Not necessarily agreement, but an assurance that Tim would try to see things from her viewpoint, that he would strive to understand her position and her experience, that he would take her side. Not in a "back me up even if I'm wrong" manner, but in an "I need to know that you're for me, as a person, as your wife" manner.

Because Tim didn't meet any of Sheila's needs, just fixes for the problems, she grew frustrated.

Behind the Lie

Why did Tim, along with so many men, act in such a dense fashion? He wasn't stupid or callous, so how did he miss meeting her needs by such a huge margin? Even though Sheila felt patronized, he didn't intend to do that. He really was trying to give her what she needed. He just responded in the way that God wired him.

First, the *task orientation* of most men predisposes them to offer answers. Men like to look at a situation and find a solution. Rather than viewing shopping as an experience to savor, they think of it as a hunting expedition. They select their target, stalk it, bag it without wasting time, and go home. Tim's favorite Christmas shopping experience came several years back when he and a friend got their lists and hit a local mall. They determined which shops would most likely have their targets, worked out an efficient route, bagged their game in half an hour, and then went to a local coffee shop for java and pie. Mission accomplished!

Sheila, however, loves to make an event of shopping. Just last Christmas, she and Teri, our daughter, met at International House of Pancakes for breakfast to connect and fortify themselves for the day. They then moseyed into Kohl's, a department store, only to get distracted by countless objects that could easily become Christmas gifts. They discussed their suitability, bought some, moved on, and even came back later to some items. Talking and being together took up most of the five hours they spent shopping, and even that wasn't enough time.

Men and women deal with problems the same way they shop. Men want solutions. Women want relationships. So when husbands encounter a problem their wives have, they know pretty quickly just what they would do to resolve the task. Creating a solution is the best way they know to help. But women don't want solutions.

But second, men are quick to offer answers because they *listen differently* than women do. Deborah Tannen wrote *You Just Don't Understand: Women and Men in Conversation,* in which she recognized the tendency of men to lecture and women to listen. Men listen for a short time and then display their knowledge and expertise, often by giving advice. Women want others to like them, so they agree and interrupt less frequently. They cherish the relationship and spending time together. These conversation styles flow from their deepest needs, which we discussed in Lie 8: Men need to feel respected, and women need to feel loved.

Men and women each look for something different in conversation. Let's not think that one is "right" and the other is "wrong." God created these differences, but we must know them so we can transcend our innate tendencies and better meet the needs of our mate.

Living the Truth

How can husbands avoid appearing to condescend to their wives? How can they give the wives what they genuinely need when they share a struggle? Let's explore two basic strategies.

Listen Differently

Joseph DeVito, in his book *Human Communication,* presents effective listening as having a number of dimensions. Each dimension has two opposite traits that exist on a continuum, and effective listening will include both traits at different times. Since men tend to lean toward one end of the continuum on several of these dimensions, emphasizing the trait they typically neglect will bring improvement in their marriages.

Empathetic and Objective Listening

Empathy focuses on understanding the other, feeling with the person. Women tend to do this better than men. They want to know how a person feels about an issue, what emotions caused the person to act in the way he or she did. They want to know if the message matches the real person. Men tend to do well at objective listening, which focuses on the facts, the problem, the solution. They want to know if the message matches reality.

Husbands will improve as they strive to increase empathy as they listen. Rather than evaluating the problem and devising solutions as they listen, they could listen more to discover what their wives felt during the event, what they're feeling as they tell the story, why they reacted the way they did.

That type of listening can be tough for men! But as husbands begin to listen with more empathy, they'll begin to understand their wives much better.

Surface and Depth Listening

Most messages have a surface meaning that comes from the literal words and grammar. Again, men pick this up pretty well, but women often include a depth message that a surface reading just won't catch. Husbands typically respond to the surface message and don't have a clue about the depth message.

When Sheila's surface message communicated the struggles at work, Tim responded to that message with solutions. But on the depth level, she wanted comfort and support. Tim never got that message until she told him directly. Men pay attention to the surface meaning but frequently miss the depth meaning.

When a wife asks, "Does this dress make me look fat?" she usually doesn't want a yes. She wants to hear that her husband thinks she looks sexy—not only in the dress she's wearing, but in anything—and that he's the luckiest guy in the world to be married to her! And men can find themselves in deep trouble when they don't seek the depth meaning.

We encourage husbands to realize that most messages have both surface and depth layers. The next time you and your wife have a conversation, probe beneath the surface. Apply your analytical skills to understand all the aspects of the message. Don't think you've understood the message if you understand the surface meaning. You've only just begun.

Since discovering that amazing, unknown world of depth meaning doesn't come naturally to most husbands, we offer the next step.

Active and Inactive Listening

Inactive listening, passively receiving the message, works well in some settings, such as college lectures. You sit there, take in the message, evaluate it, and process it. Listening to a sermon also features inactive listening. But for relationships, active listening will help husbands to get below the surface meaning and understand and empathize more.

Active listening has three components. First, *paraphrase* the speaker's meaning. Try to put what your wife said into your own words, and do it fairly objectively. Don't do it all the time, but try it when you're not sure of her meaning or when you want to show support.

Tim would have been much better off if he'd said, "So the president changed the guidelines for that contract and never told you?" That response would have given Sheila the opportunity to agree with Tim and perhaps express her feelings on the issue ("Yes! I was angry and really embarrassed when he corrected me in front of everyone!") or to correct his understanding ("Well, he told Jack, who was *supposed* to tell me, but obviously I never got the message."). Either way, Sheila would have had no doubt that Tim was listening and giving her the understanding she needed.

Second, *express understanding* of her feelings. This will get you thinking of her emotions and will let you check to see if your reading is accurate. As you echo the feelings of your wife, you give her a chance to expand on them. Sometimes she'll throw out a small hint of what's going on inside to see if it's received safely. When you express understanding, she often opens up even more.

Tim could have said, "Gosh, that must have really got you feeling frustrated, to do all that work for nothing." That one sentence has the potential to create a connection between the two of you that, to your wife, is more valuable than a diamond bracelet.

Third, *ask questions.* Probe beneath the surface. Demonstrate that you care about the deeper parts of her. Questions can clarify your understanding and get more information. Questions can move the conversation into the realm of emotions.

"So, how much time do you have now to get the project done? Is it enough?" "How did you feel when she said that?"

Husbands, you can avoid the trap of telling your wife "I know just what you need to do" when you listen in a way that shows you're willing to connect emotionally. Then you're free to move to the next step.

GIVE BIBLICAL COMFORT

When wives tell their husbands about their difficulties, they most often want some comfort and support, not advice. Four steps will help you do that.

Focus on Your Marriage

When your wife shares a work or family problem, she isn't looking for a work or family solution. She wants a marriage solution. She wants to go to the primary person in her life who will love her, accept her, support her, and strive to understand her. Most wives long for their husbands to be the type of friend revealed in Proverbs 17:17: "A friend loves at all times, and a brother is born for adversity."

In the adversity she faces, does she sense your love? Your support? Your encouragement? Are you a friend that she feels safe with when she shares her difficulties? Be that friend.

Comfort with Your Presence

Unless a person specifically asks for advice, she usually doesn't want it. Nothing is more unwanted than unsolicited advice, and husbands give it frequently! Most often, wives just need their husbands' presence and listening ear.

In the Old Testament, Job experienced difficulties beyond anything most of us will ever encounter. Three friends came to comfort him, and they gave a remarkable gift.

> When Job's three friends, Eliphaz the Temanite, Bildad the Shuhite and Zophar the Naamathite, heard about all the troubles that had come upon him, they set out from their homes and met together by agreement to go and sympathize with him and comfort him. When they saw him from a distance, they could hardly recognize him; they began to weep aloud, and they tore their robes and sprinkled dust on their heads. *Then they sat on the ground with him for seven days and seven nights. No one said a word* to him, because they saw how great his suffering was. (Job 2:11-13)

What a great example of comfort. Just being there. Not talking. Ready to listen. Expressing care. Not giving advice. Now, if you read just a little further, these men soon changed their approach, which we'll cover. But for now, focus on how they gave their presence to Job in his time of despondency.

God gave a beautiful metaphor of how to comfort with presence in Isaiah 66:12-13: "For this is what the LORD says: 'I will extend peace to her like a river ... you will nurse and be carried on her arm and dandled on her knees. As a mother comforts her child, so will I comfort you.'"

When a baby gets fussy, does a mother give advice? Usually not. She doesn't reason with the child; she picks the child up, holds her close, nurses her, and plays with her. She comforts the child with her presence.

Husbands, comfort your wives with your presence. Sit close. Give her a hug. Hold hands. Be there for her.

Seek to Understand

Transcend your innate tendency to objectively focus on the surface meaning. Try to understand what your wife experiences. Practice the active listening we mentioned. Transform your normal solution orientation into an understanding one. Put Proverbs 20:5 into practice in your marriage: "The purposes of a man's heart are deep waters, but a man of understanding draws them out."

Doesn't this verse encourage us to probe? To paraphrase? The depth meaning can be down very deep, which is, of course, why it's called *depth* meaning. Take the time, and don't accept your initial objective, surface evaluation. The more you want to understand your wife and the more you grow in understanding, the more effective you'll become at doing just that.

Give Advice with Caution

Although Job's friends began well, their strategy soon deteriorated into advice, much like Tim's suggestions to Sheila. After Job received four discouraging attempts to cheer him up, he summarized their helpfulness in this way.

> "I have heard many things like these; *miserable comforters are you all!* Will your long-winded speeches never end? What ails you that you keep on arguing? I also could speak like you, if you were in my place; I could make fine speeches against you and shake my head at you. But my mouth would encourage you; comfort from my lips would bring you relief."
> (Job 16:2-5)

Let's do a quick survey of the advice that Job's friends gave. Husbands, the next time you get tempted to offer unsolicited advice to your wives, read these and weep—and then be quiet.

1. Don't presume to give the cause. Job's friends didn't have a clue about why the bad things happened to Job. Job didn't, either. But that didn't stop the friends from giving the cause of the calamities. "Consider now: Who, being innocent, has ever perished? Where were the upright ever destroyed? As I have observed, those who plow evil and those who sow trouble reap it" (4:7-8). Job's friends were sure they had the answer Job was looking for: He had surely sinned! In truth, Job suffered because of his righteousness, not because he had plowed evil.

Husbands, avoid advice that gives the cause, especially when you don't know it for sure!

2. Don't attack spiritual maturity. One of Job's friends lauded him for his previous spirituality and good deeds, but then took it back. In effect, he said, "Job, if you were *really* mature, you could handle this better." His actual words? "But now trouble comes to you, and you are discouraged; it strikes you, and you are dismayed. Should not your piety be your confidence and your blameless ways your hope?" (4:5-6).

Husbands can slip into the danger of telling their wives that if they were just more spiritual, if they just prayed more, they could handle the situation. Husbands, if you feel tempted to say *anything* along this line, bite your tongue and give your wife a hug.

3. Don't give simplistic solutions. Another friend pretty much told Job that he'd get through okay if he just "gave it to God" and prayed about it. "But if you will look to God and plead with the Almighty, if you are pure and upright, even now he will rouse himself on your behalf and restore you to your rightful place. Your beginnings will seem humble, so prosperous will your future be" (8:5-7).

Wouldn't we love it if we could just pray to God and he'd give us all these good things? If husbands suggest their wives just give the situation to God, they make the same mistake Job's friend did.

4. Don't appear superior. As Tannen pointed out, women interpret men's lecturing and giving advice as coming across as superior. Most men don't necessarily intend to, and Tim certainly didn't with Sheila, but the wives certainly hear it that way. Job's friends did the same to him.

> "When will you end these speeches? Be sensible, and then we can talk. Why are we regarded as cattle and considered stupid in your sight?" (18:2-3)

In effect they were saying, "Job, just be quiet and listen to us. We know just what you need to do."

Husbands, we can avoid that one now, can't we?

5. Be gentle with advice. So far, we've seen examples of how *not* to give advice. But sometimes your wife may ask for a solution. Sometimes she may not ask for it, but you've built a foundation of understanding, comfort, and trust. She views you as the friend Proverbs refers to. Friends help friends, and sometimes friends have to say the hard things to other friends. When either of these occasions comes up, follow the advice from Proverbs 27:5-6: "Better is open rebuke than hidden love. Wounds from a friend can be trusted."

Husbands, be very careful in giving advice. If, however, you've built a history of comforting, listening, and supporting her, then offer your solution in love. But get past the lie that your wife needs your advice. Love her, comfort her, listen to her, support her, and you'll both benefit. And that's the truth.

Lie 11

What You Don't Know Won't Hurt You

The Truth about Transparency

We enjoy watching *Everybody Loves Raymond*, the comedy about a dysfunctional family in New York City. In one episode, friends of Ray presented an opportunity for Ray to invest in a go-kart racing track. They did the predictably goofy stunts and didn't seem at all professional, but Ray loved it and wanted to invest a thousand dollars. His wife, Deborah, saw the shabbiness of the proposal and dismissed it. Case closed, but the episode continued.

When Deborah learned that Ray had invested the money without her knowledge or consent, she hit the roof; a family fracas ensued in which she berated his lack of openness with her. She talked at length about how couples should share the important issues with one another, but she got exceptionally silent after she accidentally revealed that she'd borrowed a thousand dollars from Ray's mom several years before and never told him. Openness in marriage really should involve both partners!

In researching this book and in conversations with couples over the years, we've been amazed at how often husbands keep secrets from their wives. Big secrets, little secrets. But secrets nonetheless. Secrets that impact the marriage.

Both of the following stories come from actual couples, although we've changed many of the details to protect their privacy.

Brad got a bug for a new car. His older, paid-off Taurus still ran well and looked pretty good, but he wanted an Escalade, the Cadillac SUV. He spent some time looking around, found a great deal through the Internet, and proudly brought it home to show it off. Monica, who paid the bills, knew they couldn't afford the four-hundred-dollar payment every month. He kept the secret of wanting a new car; he kept the secret of looking for a new car—until he couldn't keep it secret any longer.

Bryan topped Brad. His company relocated him to the Bay area in northern California from Atlanta on fairly short notice, and Melanie stayed behind for a few months to finish all the details while he worked out housing arrangements. They decided to rent a house until they knew the area a little better. But the 20 percent annual appreciation of housing costs made Bryan fear they'd lose too much ground, so he bought a house. He did his homework, and he got a good deal on a nice home. He neglected, however, to tell Melanie about his purchase until she arrived, ready to move in to their rental.

Perhaps because he hadn't told her, perhaps because she simply didn't want a two-story house, she never connected with it. Six months later they sold the house to buy another one, but they lost $25,000 on the closing costs.

The Lie

Too often, husbands keep secrets from their wives because they believe that what she doesn't know won't hurt her. They assume she'll never find out. Other times they operate under the premise that "it's easier to ask forgiveness than permission." They know the secret will come out, but they want what they want, so rather than work it out first and perhaps lose the chance, they go ahead and don't tell until they have to.

Both beliefs are lies. Both damage the oneness that God designed for marriage. Both move the couple further apart rather than closer together.

On the Receiving End

Since we used three stories to begin the chapter, we can't easily focus on what just one wife felt. But let's explore some typical reactions of wives when they discover their husbands have kept secrets.

MARRIAGE ROLE MINIMIZED

When a wife finds out that her husband has kept a secret from her, she suddenly feels as if she is less than a full partner in her marriage. Her feeling increases when the secret deals with a mutual concern, such as buying a house or car. She loses her sense of participating in the marriage; she feels that her husband wants to limit her input and assumes he doesn't value what she brings to the relationship. She feels devalued when he goes behind her back to get what he wants. Why did he? He knew that she wouldn't agree.

RESENTMENT

Keeping secrets also leads to resentment within the wife. Resentment at her husband's lack of spiritual leadership and his lack of integrity, not to mention his childish behavior. Her resentment can easily spill over into other dimensions of the relationship. Her husband took something of value from her, and she feels not only the specific loss, but also the loss of respect for her husband.

RESISTANCE

Melanie's reaction to her husband's revealed secret was resistance. When Bryan purchased the home without her knowing it, he created a built-in resistance to the house. She had no role in picking it out, so she felt no sense of ownership and no sense of partnership with her husband. Some details of the house just didn't match her desires, but that was secondary to her. Ironically, she could have lived with some of those details if she had participated in the decision. She also noticed her resistance spilling over into her general attitude toward him. Over time, she came to resist more and more of his desires because she feared he might do something like this again. She didn't trust him as much, so she dug in her heels in a number of areas: the type of food she prepared for them, the style of clothing she wore, even the frequency of their lovemaking.

DISTANCE

The perceived closeness between a husband and wife will typically suffer when significant secrets come out. Because the wife's role has been minimized, because both resentment and resistance live within her mind, she can't feel as close to the man she once trusted implicitly. She often perceives the secret as her husband's desire to move away from intimacy and transparency.

Behind the Lie

Let's explore some of the typical secrets men keep and why they keep them.

WHAT MEN HIDE

At the risk of sounding too simplistic, men tend to hide everything. Very little escapes the masculine tendency to keep secrets. And at the core, men hide the truth. They conceal the full story. Not all men. Not always. But too many and too often.

❖ Men hide *finances*, as illustrated by Brad and Bryan. They hide purchases, loans they've given or received, or even the general state of the family finances. In his years of ministry, Tim encountered situations in which when a husband died and his wife had no clue about their financial condition. One wife had to sell the house, rent an apartment, and get a job, even though they'd lived well before the man's death. Another wife bought a Mercedes and began to travel when she discovered the truth!

❖ Men hide their *accomplishments*. Granted, some never shut up about them, but others feel uneasy talking about their successes and keep them to themselves.

✤ Men hide their *attraction to other women,* as we discussed in Lies 2 and 3. Perhaps they don't want to acknowledge it, perhaps they don't want to stop it, perhaps they don't want to make their wives feel uncomfortable. Or maybe they want to make their wives feel uneasy because that gives them a sense of control.

✤ Men hide their *activities.* Their schedules, plans, and actions often don't get expressed. Or they pop an activity on their wives, convinced they mentioned it two weeks before, even though they never even gave a hint.

✤ Men hide their *wrongs.* We explored this in Lie 9 and will touch on it again in the next lie.

✤ Men hide their *health issues.* We looked at this in Lie 6 and saw how men find it difficult to face and admit problems with their health.

Now, do you see why we said men will hide almost anything? But why don't they just tell the truth?

Why Men Hide

In part, men hide because they're men. They tend to be more quiet and less relational than women. They use fewer words in a day. Their streak of independence encourages self-containment, keeping something in reserve. They fear the loss of control that transparency can bring.

Joseph DeVito, in the book we mentioned earlier, *Human Communication,* cites several studies that indicate that women generally disclose much more than men. While women often self-disclose negative emotions, men rarely do, either to other men or to women. So part of the reticence husbands feel comes from their masculinity.

They also avoid disclosure when they know they've done wrong. As we discussed in Lie 9, the masculine need for respect can make it difficult to acknowledge wrongdoing. It shatters the image that many men want to project.

Perhaps the greatest reason men keep secrets comes from their recognizing the dangers of disclosure. When we share, we make ourselves more vulnerable. We face more risks. Particularly, we face more relational risks, an area in which men don't feel particularly competent. Disclosure requires that we trust the person we disclose to.

Even Jesus hesitated to disclose too much. Early in his ministry, many saw his miracles and believed in him. Exciting stuff! But notice Jesus' response: "Now while he was in Jerusalem at the Passover Feast, many people saw the miraculous signs he was doing and believed in his name. But Jesus *would not entrust himself to them,* for he knew all men. He did not need man's testimony about man, for he knew what was in a man" (John 2:23-25). The New Living Translation renders that last verse this way: "No one needed to tell him about human nature."

Transparency requires trust, and human nature isn't fully trustworthy. Disclosing the truth carries the risk of rejection. The wife may lose respect for her husband. She may become resentful or resistant. These losses may be temporary or they may endure for the rest of the marriage. They may even lead to the dissolution of the marriage. But all these reasons combine to make many husbands leery of telling the truth, the whole truth, and nothing but the truth. Instead, they keep secrets. How can they move toward transparency?

Living the Truth

Husbands, we recognize that a great inertia exists when it comes to making a commitment to live transparently with your wife. Husbands don't easily begin disclosing what they've kept hidden. Even Jesus encouraged people to carefully consider the cost of any course of action.

"Suppose one of you wants to build a tower. Will he not first sit down and *estimate the cost* to see if he has enough money to complete it? For if he lays the foundation and is not able to finish it, everyone who sees it will ridicule him." (Luke 14:28–29)

Let's look at the considerable costs of keeping secrets.

✢ You have *less connection* with your wives. Even independent men want connection with their wives—emotionally, intellectually, spiritually, and physically. Keeping secrets walls off part of your lives, your wives can't participate in those areas, and your connection decreases.

✢ You can't escape the *fear of them finding out*. That fear can eat away at you and take away the ease of being together. Any conversation can be the one that brings your secret into the open, so you tend to avoid talking.

✢ Keeping the secret won't shield you from the *consequences of the act* you hide. Those consequences can bring the secret out into the open. Earvin "Magic" Johnson took advantage of the numerous sexual opportunities available to professional basketball players, and his wife never had a clue. He kept the secret until he acquired HIV, the precursor to AIDS.

✢ And, you face the *consequences of hiding* the truth. You'll feel the tension of pretending. Your closeness with your wife will decrease when you choose not to trust her with the truth. And not only does the level of connection decrease, the act of hiding truth can even lead to the end of marriage. Many women struggle more to get over the deception than the act, because deception strikes at the heart of marriage.

So, husbands, as you look at the secrets you keep, know the cost of continuing. Once you count the cost and discover the price is higher than you want to pay, then you can take the next step.

TARGET TRANSPARENCY

Transparency plays more of a role in life than we sometimes like to think. We like to believe we have privacy, but with God, we have no privacy at all. Despite our attempts to keep secrets, we have none from God. Hebrews 4:12–13 tells us,

> For the word of God is living and active. Sharper than any double-edged sword, it penetrates even to dividing soul and spirit, joints and marrow; it judges the thoughts and attitudes of the heart. Nothing in all creation is hidden from God's sight. *Everything is uncovered and laid bare before the eyes of him* to whom we must give account.

Let's think about using these verses as a pattern for our lives. Transparency. Openness. Not keeping secrets. Not deceiving. With God, transparency is full reality. With humans, transparency is a goal, the direction we choose to move. Rather than moving away from openness, we can move closer. Husbands, particularly, need to move in that direction with their wives.

God designed marriage for an open sharing that flows from how he created mankind.

> So the LORD God caused a deep sleep to fall upon the man, and he slept; then He took one of his ribs and closed up the flesh at that place. The Lord God *fashioned into a woman the rib which He had taken from the man*, and brought her to the man. The man said, "This is now bone of my bones, And flesh of my flesh; She shall be called Woman, Because she was taken out of Man." For this reason a man shall leave his father and his mother, and be *joined*

to his wife; and they shall become *one flesh*."
And the man and his wife were both *naked
and were not ashamed*. (Gen. 2:21–25 NASB)

First, woman comes from the very substance of man.
Perhaps our mutual attraction represents an innate yearning to
reconnect what once was one. Second, marriage joins two
separate individuals into one flesh, into one shared life. When
Sheila's fibromyalgia flares up, it impacts the functioning of her
entire body. In the same way, whatever impacts the husband
will impact the wife, since they're one body. How can we keep
secrets from ourselves? That violates the marriage design.

Third, in marriage the husband and wife are naked and not
ashamed. The obvious meaning certainly includes the physical.
We don't want to minimize that, but nakedness goes deeper.
Metaphorically, clothing hides the real us. In marriage, we should
work toward eliminating anything that keeps our mate from
seeing us as we really are.

Secrets. Truth that we hide. A good marriage moves closer
to the original design of openness. Notice that verb "moves."
Becoming transparent is a process. We don't do it instantly and
fully.

BUILD TRANSPARENCY

Becoming transparent is an ongoing process that requires
building trust within a marriage. Sure, we'd love for it to be
instantaneous, but it just doesn't work that way. We don't open
up to people we don't feel safe with, and husbands already
struggle to open up with people they *do* feel safe with. Over
time and by our actions, we prove to each other that we're
worthy of the other person's trust, that helping them to feel
secure is important to us.

God develops trust in us the same way. He gives us small
responsibilities, and if we act in a trustworthy manner, he gives
us greater responsibilities, and so on. Jesus explained the
process.

> "Whoever can be trusted with very little can also
> be trusted with much, and whoever is dishonest

with very little will also be dishonest with much. So if you have not been trustworthy in handling worldly wealth, who will trust you with true riches? And if you have not been trustworthy with someone else's property, who will give you property of your own?" (Luke 16:10–12)

The principle of building trust in small steps certainly applies to handling truth. If a husband has a history of hiding, we don't necessarily recommend that he sit down with his wife and reveal everything. That may not be appropriate, wise, or safe. But he can begin moving in the direction of disclosure. Test the waters. Pray and seek spiritual counsel.

The wives can do much to build a safe environment that enhances openness. Since husbands typically find it difficult to be straightforward, do what you can to make it easier. They have a responsibility to move toward openness, and you have a responsibility to make it safer for them.

DeVito gives four guidelines on responding to disclosure that can help wives. These guidelines don't deal with how to handle the content of what husbands reveal, just how to help them express more truth.

1. Listen actively. Listen for different levels of meaning, especially for what may lurk beneath the surface. When you think you might hear something, clarify your conclusions with questions. Try to understand his viewpoint, even if you don't agree with it. Paraphrase his message back to him to ensure you heard it correctly.

2. Support him. Try not to evaluate and judge too much in the early stages. Verbalize your gladness that he did share. Let him set the pace; don't unnecessarily speed up the encounter. Try to listen empathetically. Remember that the two of you are connected.

3. Maintain confidentiality. Support groups recite this phrase at the end of their meetings: "What's said here stays here." That assurance creates a safe environment. Nothing will kill transparency more than telling what's been revealed in private. Yes, these revelations can make great stories, but until your husband says it in a public setting, you shouldn't either.

4. Don't use disclosures as weapons. When your husband discloses a weakness, something he's done wrong, or a vulnerability, you have a powerful weapon available. Lose your arsenal. If you use his words against him, you've betrayed the trust he put in you by disclosing to you.

Practicing each of these four steps will help your husband feel like you want him to share and that he's safe to share with you. Paul gave a goal in Titus 2:10 that certainly applies to building transparency in marriages: "Show that they can be fully trusted." Wives, you may be fully trustworthy, but your husband needs to learn that by experience.

Now, let's look at two specific questions focusing on how couples handle transparency.

WHAT SHOULD COUPLES SHARE?

We're going to skate on this one. The level of transparency depends on each couple, their history, their personalities, and how safe an environment they can build. But we strongly give two principles that serve as default settings.

First, don't deceive. Don't tell untruths. You may not yet be able to reveal everything, but don't deceive. Ephesians 4:25 says, "Therefore each of you must *put off falsehood* and *speak truthfully* to his neighbor, for we are all members of one body." Put off falsehood and deception. Speak the truth.

Husbands, when you demonstrate this to your wives, they'll begin to trust your honesty more. Their suspicion will decrease. That in turn will make it a little easier for you to share more. Do this because it's the right thing. That leads to our second default setting.

Move toward truth and transparency. We recognize this is a process; trust and safety have to exist. But move in the direction of openness. I (Tim) recently had a terrible dream dealing with my dad and our cat, a dream that in no way matched Dad, the cat, or reality. I really hesitated to share the dream with Sheila. Would she think I was a sick person for even dreaming what I did? I took a chance and told her about it, she handled it well, I felt much better to get it expressed, and now I feel more confident about sharing other difficult issues.

HOW SHOULD WIVES RESPOND?

As couples move into transparency, difficult issues will arise. Sins come out. Vulnerabilities get revealed. Some dark perspectives become known. Again, each situation requires a different response, based on the couple, the setting, the history, and all. But again, we suggest two default settings.

First, focus on grace and forgiveness. Remember that the overall goal is to improve the marriage, and forgiveness must flow in both directions. Don't ignore sinful behavior, but extend grace. Jesus showed the importance of forgiving with grace.

> "Do to others as you would have them do to you. …
>
> But love your enemies, do good to them, and lend to them without expecting to get anything back. Then your reward will be great, and you will be sons of the Most High, because he is kind to the ungrateful and wicked. *Be merciful*, just as your Father is merciful.
>
> *Do not judge*, and you will not be judged. *Do not condemn*, and you will not be condemned. *Forgive*, and you will be forgiven." (Luke 6:31, 35-37)

Jesus conditioned our receiving mercy and forgiveness— and avoiding judgment and condemnation—on our willingness to treat others in the way we desire to be treated. So, wives, extend mercy and forgiveness to your husbands when they make those disclosures about wrongs they've done.

Second, focus on restoration. Avoid the blame game. Look at how to move on from where you are now. Deal with the issues involved with the purpose of eliminating them from your future. Those issues may include hurt and anger, which can be tough to face. Work through the feelings anyway. Don't look backwards except with forgiveness. Allow the relationship to recover.

Didn't Jesus make that point with the story of the prodigal son? The son wronged the father and then recognized his sin. He returned, knowing he no longer deserved to be a son. When the father saw his son and his genuine repentance, he immediately restored the family relationship.

> "Quick! Bring the best robe and put it on him. Put a ring on his finger and sandals on his feet. Bring the fattened calf and kill it. Let's have a feast and celebrate. For this son of mine was dead and is alive again; he was lost and is found." So they began to celebrate. (Luke 15:22–24)

Isn't that the goal of transparency? The restoration of family relationships? That's progress worth celebrating.

Husbands, we talked earlier about headship, that husbands have a spiritual responsibility to move the family in a godly direction. Transparency *is* godly. Take the initiative, as difficult as that can be. Be strong. Be manly. Move toward transparency. And as you do, you'll work through difficulties, you'll see obstacles decreased, and both you and your wife will benefit. And that's the truth.

Lie 12

All You Do Is Nag

The Truth about Accountability

Ralph and Karla saw an excellent premarital counselor from their church. He helped them work through expectations and desires and what roles they each anticipated they would play. One issue centered on who would handle the finances. Karla's dad took care of the money in her family, and she expected Ralph to do the same. But Ralph's mom did that in his family, and he expected Karla to follow suit. After they discussed the matter, Ralph pledged to do it.

And he did—for a couple of years. But slowly, he shifted many of the responsibilities over to Karla. At first, he asked her to keep track of the credit-card receipts and reconcile them with the monthly statement. She didn't particularly like doing that, so perhaps that's why she didn't do a good job. Eventually she asked, with a touch of frustration in her voice, if he could take the responsibility back. When she didn't get the response she wanted, she asked several more times.

"Karla, do you have to keep nagging about that? I could use some help here. Don't just think of yourself."

Not long after, he had to go on a business trip during the same week he paid the bills, so he asked her to do it that month. Just that month. On his return, she nagged at him to take it back, and he grudgingly agreed. But the next month found another excuse, and he thought that paying bills fit in with reconciling the credit cards, and he was pretty busy.

She noticed, though, that the night she paid the bills, he watched the Phoenix Suns basketball game. Her resentment grew with each check she signed. She couldn't keep the shrewish tone out of her voice when she said, "I don't know why you can't just do *all* the finances for us. You agreed to in premarital, remember?"

"All you do is nag, nag, nag. Can't you get off my back a little? I do the best I can."

This cycle continued. Ralph would gradually shift more to her, she'd nag about it, and they'd both get frustrated. Every time Karla mentioned the bills, he'd mention the nagging. He soon discovered his response worked great at getting the focus off what he didn't do.

The Lie

When wives confront their husbands about something they've done that they shouldn't have, or something they've not done that they should have, husbands often evade the issue by attacking the nagging that their wives do. They hope to either divert or deny the issue and thus escape their own responsibility.

When husbands say, "All you do is nag. Can't you get off my back?" they lie. They try to escape the truth about their own behavior.

On the Receiving End

Karla thought Ralph was lazy, that he just didn't want to put the time into managing their finances when he could be watching sports on TV. So she got angry at him when he got angry at her for nagging. She knew she nagged; she just couldn't let go of the issue. To her, his behavior reflected a lack of integrity; he'd promised to do the finances before they got married, and now he wasn't following through. She wondered how a Christian man could go back on his word and not be bothered by it. She felt that he didn't care about her concerns or his commitments. Even though Ralph has shown no desire to live up to his commitment, she still wants to forgive him. But she struggles with doing so, and she's begun to question how much he cares about her altogether. A sense of betrayal lurks fairly close to the surface. And because she can't let go of the issue, she continues to nag at him, which, to her surprise, seems to work! At least on a short-term basis. She's discovered that her nagging can make him uncomfortable enough that he changes, for a while. Pretty soon, though, he goes back to the old ways, she gets more frustrated, she nags more, he changes, and the cycle begins again.

She discovered the secret that Delilah found with Samson: Nagging works! One day while reading in Judges, Karla came across 16:16. Delilah asked Samson to reveal the source of his strength, but he kept giving false leads. She wouldn't give up wanting to know the truth. "*With such nagging she prodded him day after day until he was tired to death.*" The nagging got Samson to tell her the truth, and she betrayed him. As a result, he lost his strength, his enemies captured him, and he eventually died. Truly, she nagged him to death.

But Karla didn't want to nag Ralph to death; she just wanted him to take care of the finances!

Behind the Lie

Why do men resist being nagged by their wives? Several reasons exist why men evade issues.

No Desire to Change

Ralph didn't change because he truly didn't want to do the finances. He felt Karla had pushed him into it in the first place. Like many husbands, he grudgingly agreed just to keep the peace, but he planned on changing things after a while.

This lack of desire to change behavior may involve issues that husbands have agreed to that don't have any innate moral implication, like with Karla and Ralph. It may involve issues that have a moral component, perhaps looking at other women, as we discussed in Lies 2 and 3. Wives see a problem in the behavior and bring it up, and the husbands either deny or divert the discussion. They take the focus away from themselves and turn it on the wife's nagging. In truth, they don't want to change.

STRUGGLE WITH CHANGE

Sometimes a husband knows he needs to do something, and he makes a sincere attempt, but he just can't quite build a consistent habit. So when his wife points out his failing, he doesn't want to acknowledge it and then evades the truth by talking about her nagging. If he diverts the issue to her nagging, then his failure won't draw as much fire.

NAGGING BACKFIRES

Karla discovered that in the early stages, nagging seemed to work. If she didn't say anything, Ralph's unwanted behavior continued and sometimes got worse. If she nagged, he would change. Like Samson, Ralph gave in, overwhelmed by her greater number of words and desperate to get her off his back.

Still, he resented the nagging, and he resented the fact that he had to give in to keep peace in the family, so he tuned her out. He paid as little attention to her as he could get by with when she went on her rampages.

Ironically, that led Karla to ramp up the nagging even more. Just like a drug addict needs more dope to get the high, Karla had to nag more to get the response. So Ralph resisted more, she nagged more, and again the cycle spiraled downward.

Neither read the numerous verses in Proverbs that indicate nagging doesn't work for long.

> "A nagging wife annoys like a constant dripping" (19:13 NLT).

> "It is better to live alone in the corner of an attic than with a contentious wife in a lovely home" (21:9 NLT).

> "It is better to live alone in the desert than with a crabby, complaining wife" (21:19 NLT).

"A nagging wife is as annoying as the constant dripping on a rainy day. Trying to stop her complaints is like trying to stop the wind or hold something with greased hands" (27:15-16 NLT).

If Ralph had ever read those verses, he would have printed them out on parchment paper, framed them, and given them to Karla. He didn't particularly like doing the finances for her, but he especially didn't want to get pushed into it by her nagging. He longed for a better way to resolve the issues.

Living the Truth

Four steps can help husbands increase their willingness to face issues their wives have, without resorting to the lie, "All you do is nag."

UNDERSTAND ACCOUNTABILITY

We take significant steps toward living in the truth when we determine to be accountable to people with whom we have a strong relationship. We don't necessarily have to give an account for our behavior to a person we barely know and have never influenced. But the closer we get to a person, the more accountable we are to him or her.

None of us has full freedom to do just as we desire. Our behavior impacts others. As a philosopher said, "Your right to extend your fist ends several inches in front of my nose." And if the person extends his fist to contact the nose, you know he's going to give an account.

Accountability has four primary dimensions. First, we're *accountable to God* for what we do with our lives, our time, our gifts, and our energy. "So then, each of us will give an account of himself to God" (Rom. 14:12).

Second, we're *accountable to society and the government* to carry out the laws of the land. "For rulers hold no terror for those who do right, but for those who do wrong. Do you want to be free from fear of the one in authority? Then do what is right and he will commend you" (Rom. 13:3).

Third, each Christian is *accountable to fellow Christians*. If one follower of Christ sees another doing something wrong, he's responsible to go to the person. "Brothers, if someone is caught in a sin, you who are spiritual should restore him gently. But watch yourself, or you also may be tempted" (Gal. 6:1). Christians are connected to one another and they need to involve themselves in each other's lives.

Fourth, and most relevant to our discussion, husbands are *accountable to their wives.* We have two reasons for that. First, if both claim Christ, then they're accountable as brother and sister in Christ. But we can go deeper, as we look back at the passage that described headship in marriage, Ephesians 5:25-28.

> Husbands, love your wives, just as Christ loved the church and gave himself up for her to *make her holy*, cleansing her by the washing with water through the word, and to present her to himself as a radiant church, *without stain or wrinkle or any other blemish*, but holy and blameless. In this same way, husbands ought to love their wives as their own bodies. He who loves his wife loves himself.

Husbands should build up their wives, just as Christ did for the church. If a husband isn't doing the job, doesn't it make sense that she let him know? That's a good example of husbandly accountability to their wives. What does that mean? Very simply, wives can call husbands to account. If the husband's behavior is problematic, either morally or based on an agreement between them, then the wife can validly bring it up.

Accountability in itself is not nagging or getting on his back. Now, wives *can* take valid accountability into nagging, but that's another issue! Our issue is how husbands focus on the wives' nagging to avoid dealing with issues. Understanding and accepting that they are accountable to their wives begins the process of living in the truth.

ACCOUNTABILITY INVOLVES CONFRONTATION

Confrontation is what distinguishes accountability from nagging. Confrontation, or as some call it "care-frontation," deals with issues in a godly, frank, gracious manner. Guess that leaves out nagging, doesn't it! Let's explore just one passage that explores confrontation, Galatians 6:1-2: "Brothers, if someone is *caught in a sin*, you who are *spiritual* should restore him *gently*. But watch yourself, or you also may be tempted. *Carry each other's burdens*, and in this way you will fulfill the law of Christ."

Let's assume the husband sins. The wife, with spiritual concern for him, confronts him in a gentle manner. Her motivation is to help him with the burden of the sin—not to nag, not to judge him, but to help. They deal with the sin constructively and graciously. The husband is restored, and the marriage is strengthened as trust is built.

(If you want to explore confrontation a little more, please read Leviticus 19:17, Matthew 18:15-17, and Luke 17:3-4.)

We think that both wives and husbands can benefit by thinking carefully about biblical confrontation, but the next step belongs to the husbands alone.

DESIRE CONFRONTATION

Wanting confrontation sounds stupid, doesn't it? And it is, if husbands want to continue in behavior that makes life more difficult for their wives. But if husbands want to grow in godliness and create an effective marriage, then they must desire that their inadequacies get pointed out—in love.

David learned this principle, as he told us in Psalm 141:5: "Let the godly strike me! It will be a kindness! If they reprove me, it is soothing medicine. Don't let me refuse it." David wanted godly people to tell him about his sins. What a tremendous example for husbands! Why then do they accuse their wives of nagging in an attempt to excuse themselves?

The poet Robert Burns wrote, "Oh would some power the good Lord give us, to see ourselves as others see us."

Care-frontation does that. We all have blind spots—faults and weaknesses that we can't see—until someone close, who loves us, points them out with grace. And grace makes all the difference. Husbands, when your wives point out what they see as a problem, welcome what they say. View it as a chance to see yourself from another's eyes. View it as a chance to learn how to better meet the needs of your wives.

Listen honestly. Evaluate their words. You might even talk to others to get their perspective. Listen empathetically to see it from their viewpoint. Even if your wives speak in white-hot anger, or while frozen in resentment, listen for whatever truth may be there. Ask God for wisdom to discern the truth, to determine the best way to proceed.

And don't accuse them of nagging. Don't try to evade the issue. As you willingly face the concerns of your wives, you'll find good things happening. Your wives will trust you more. They'll nag less. You'll become more godly. You'll become better husbands. And that's the truth.

Readers' Guide

For Personal Reflection or Group Discussion

Readers' Guide

The following questions are based on the chapters in this book. They offer you, your spouse, and possibly a small group of married couples the opportunity to delve more deeply into essential points drawn from each chapter. As you explore them and apply what you learn, you will reap positive benefits that result when truth is valued and applied to everyday situations.

Yes, thinking through these questions—and issues they may raise—will require commitment, courage, and perseverance. It will take time to work through some of these issues with your spouse, especially if unresolved conflicts exist in your marriage. But the results will be worth it! (Note to guys: Rise up to meet this challenge—for your own good, the well-being of your spouse, and the health of your marriage. Don't say, "I don't need to do this today; I'll do it another time." Start today.)

No matter how great or less-than-great your marriage may be, God is ready to work in your life! He wants to help you make your marriage the best it can be. And the more honest you are— with yourself, with God, with your spouse, and perhaps with other couples in a "safe" environment—the more benefits you will reap.

Recognizing that husbands and wives often view the same situations in completely different ways, the first questions for each chapter are designed for you and/or your spouse to answer and hopefully discuss together. Specific *Reflections* questions for each of you to consider follow. You may choose to discuss them with your spouse, but primarily they are for *you* alone.

Feel free to adapt these questions for your personal use or for the unique requirements of your small group. You may, for example, choose to delve more deeply into a particular topic or spend quite a bit of time on one or two questions. You may discuss one chapter a week or spend several weeks on a chapter. You may work through these questions on your own, but whenever possible, we encourage you to use and discuss them with your spouse. (Due to issues of vulnerability, some questions suitable for you and/or your spouse may not be appropriate to discuss in a group setting.)

Be encouraged by the small but significant improvements that occur in your marriage when you start discussing and applying principles from this book. Ask God to open your eyes to new ideas, new ways of responding to your spouse, and ways in which you can improve your relationship with your spouse. God will multiply your efforts and those of your spouse. Transparency and love can replace "untruths" that have taken root, deliberately or accidentally.

Just like we did, you *can* build an even stronger marriage foundation—one truth at a time. Remember, God is faithful and "able to do immeasurably more than all we ask or imagine, according to his power that is at work within us" (Eph. 3:20).

LIE 1

1. What did you think and feel as you read about Dennis and Carol's marriage? How did Dennis express his love for Carol? Why did she feel cheated and lied to despite his efforts?

2. What does the word *cherish* mean?

3. What was your courtship like? What special things did you do for the one who later became your spouse? Since your wedding

    a. how have you continued to demonstrate your commitment to love and cherish your spouse?

    b. which responsibilities, choices, relationships, etc., have negatively affected your commitment to love and cherish your spouse? (Be honest!)

4. What do Genesis 2:21-25 and Song of Songs 2:3-6 and 8:6 reveal about a wife's need to be cherished? About the husband's need to meet that need?

5. Reread Ephesians 5:25-33. What kind of a standard does God set for husbands?

6. Do you agree that husbands' degree of sacrifice for their wives exhibits the value they place on their wives? Why or why not?

7. When wives don't feel cherished, how do they respond? What serious consequences can occur when husbands do not meet their wives' needs?

Reflections for the Husband

1. Think about the four steps you can take in order to live in the truth of meeting your wife's needs to be cherished:

    a. realize the need;

b. ask your wife which specific acts make her feel cherished;

c. do some of those specific acts for your wife; and

d. tell your wife she's special.

2. How can you begin to practice these four steps? Which challenges will you face as you begin to practice these?

3. Reread the authors' suggestions on special acts you can do for your wife. How can you begin to practice some of these, starting today?

Reflections for the Wife

1. The fifth step encourages you to realize that "men are men." What can you do to give your husband credit for things he does *from his perspective* to cherish you? To show appreciation for acts he does in response to your requests?

LIE 2

1. Why is the lie "all men look at women" so damaging?

2. Which emotions assail wives whose husbands look at other women lustfully? What happens to marital relationships when wives feel vulnerable because of their husbands' lust and seek to protect themselves?

3. Reread Matthew 5:27–28 and Hebrews 4:15. What is the difference between sexual temptation and sexual sin?

4. Which two components, according to the authors, comprise "lustful looking"?

5. Why, according to Job 31:1–4 and Isaiah 59:2, is lustful looking so dangerous? Consider its effects on such areas as

a. the lustful husband's relationship with his wife—including their sexual intimacy; and

b. the lustful husband's relationship with God.

6. Do you agree or disagree with this sentence: "The more a man lusts, the stronger the lustful desire becomes"? Why or why not?

Reflections for the Husband

1. In what way(s) might you, or someone you know, be minimizing the dangers of lustful looking? Why is lust so easy to rationalize?

2. What do the following verses reveal about how each of us can build new patterns of thinking and behavior and find victory over lust?

   a. Proverbs 4:25-27

   b. Romans 8:5-8

   c. Job 31:1

   d. James 5:16

   e. 1 John 1:8-9

3. When are you most vulnerable to lustful looking? What steps can you take to avoid most visual temptations? Are you willing to take these steps? Why or why not?

4. Why can lustful looking become addictive?

Reflections for the Wife

1. How might you respond if you discover your husband is involved in lustful looking?

2. When might it be appropriate for you to read *Every Man's Battle* (Stoeker and Arterburn) or other Christian books dealing with sexual temptation, pornography, and/or sexual addiction?

3. With whom might you be able to talk about your husband's lust and its impact on you and your family? Why is it important to talk about lustful looking with at least one other female friend rather than keeping your emotions bottled up inside?

4. Why do you think the authors encourage men to talk about their lust-related battles with other men, at least at first, rather than sharing first with their wives?

LIE 3

1. Why do you think Tony kept Joan's letters and continued to connect with her? Why is "an affair of the heart" a deep threat to a marriage, even when the affair is not sexual?

2. What happens when a husband denies—to himself or others—that he feels an attraction to another woman in a romantic, relational, or sexual manner?

3. Do you think that Tony lied to Debbie by continuing his friendship with Joan, or was he innocent of deceit? What role did his memories play, and why did he protect the special "secrets" of what went on between him and Joan years earlier?

4. Which unmet needs make husbands more vulnerable to the attraction of other women? What types of things can happen when husbands with unmet needs "open the door" to having those needs met through relationships with women other than their spouses?

5. According to the authors, why do many husbands avoid telling their wives that they are attracted to other women?

6. What does God say about the importance of faithfully keeping our marriage vows—the covenant we each have made with our spouse? (See Mal. 2:14–15.) What does it mean to "break faith" with a spouse?

7. Why is moving in the direction of principled honesty a necessary part of fidelity?

8. What does Proverbs 5:3–8 reveal about the attractions and dangers of an inappropriate relationship with someone other than your spouse?

Reflections for the Husband

1. Examine relationships you have with other women—neighbors, co-workers, extended family members, etc. Do any of them pose potential risk to you and your marriage? If so, what battle strategy do you need to implement?

2. How honest are you being with God concerning any temptation to be unfaithful?

3. With which male person(s) can you be scrupulously honest and transparent, building spiritual accountability into your life? (See James 5:16.)

4. What might you be able to do, given your relationship with your wife, to move toward deeper honesty with her when you find yourself attracted to another woman?

5. In practical terms, what does it mean to value your wife above everything and everyone except God?

6. To what extent are you willing to "run" from any relationship that might harm your marriage, regardless of what the cost to you may be?

7. Are you willing to use the six "hedges" mentioned in this chapter? If not, why not? If yes, how can you begin implementing them *today*?

Reflections for the Wife

1. Have you felt threatened by your husband's outside relationship with another woman? If so, how did you respond? How might you communicate your sensitivity to your husband, who may not understand why you even perceive a problem?

2. Review the six "hedges" that can help to protect your marriage, and substitute the words "man" and "husband" for "woman" and "wife" so that the hedges apply to your relationship with any man who is not your husband.

Lie 4

1. When the word *submission* is mentioned today, how do people generally respond (especially married women)? Why? How have views of marital roles changed within the last fifty years?

2. What is the difference between leadership and domination?

3. What did you think about as you read the four consequences of sin that affect oneness in marriage—shame, blame, wife's desire to dominate, husband's rule? To what extent do you see each of these exhibited in your marriage? In the marriages of others?

4. What do the following verses reveal about God's blueprint for marriage?

   a. Genesis 2:21-25

   b. Ephesians 5:18, 21

5. Read the biblical pattern found in Ephesians 5:23-30.

   a. In what ways is this pattern different from other patterns?

b. Who is the biblical example of headship, the one whom headship is patterned after?

c. What is the relationship between headship and sacrifice (5:23-24)?

d. What responsibility does headship entail (5:25-27)?

Reflections for the Husband

1. What practical things can you do to demonstrate your love for your wife? To sacrifice for her? To encourage her to develop her gifts and abilities?

Reflections for the Wife

1. Do you view your husband as the head of your family? Why or why not?

2. How might you and your husband better apply the biblical patterns of headship, submission, love, and sacrifice in your marriage?

3. What can you do to encourage your husband to be the sacrificial, loving leader God calls him to be?

LIE 5

1. In the story at the beginning of this chapter, why did Jason keep postponing Traci's to-do projects? Why did Traci become frustrated with Jason? What factors caused them to become trapped in a downward cycle of resentment, nagging, and frustration?

2. Which of the reasons behind why husbands often say, "I'll get to it next week," resonated with you? Why?

3. Generally speaking, how do wives' views of their homes differ from the views of their husbands?

4. Which point(s) in Philippians 2:3–4 stood out to you? Why?

5. "Strive for understanding and empathy," the authors wrote, and then urged readers to be willing to make changes they need to make rather than primarily focusing on changes the other person needs to make. What does this perspective accomplish?

6. How might you implement a "to-do plan" that contains the following?

   a. a list of projects that need to be completed, in priority order

   b. accurate time parameters

   c. appreciation of what each of you accomplishes

Reflections for the Husband and the Wife to Read Separately

1. How well do you communicate about "to-do" lists and priorities?

2. In what way(s) might mutual submission benefit both of you?

3. Why is it important for both of you to share desires and frustrations related to "to-do" projects?

4. Which "ground rules" might be valuable to use during your discussions?

5. In the end, is getting projects done the most important thing? What other things might be more important for both of you to learn?

Lie 6

1. Why do so many men (and women) put off dealing with health-related issues and minimize their physical problems? What are some common excuses?

2. How might Karen have handled discussions with Rick differently, especially when his denials contradicted the warning signals she recognized? Have some of her concerns surfaced in your marriage, too? If so, which ones?

3. What's the balance between being manly (1 Kings 2:2; Proverbs 20:29) and being stupid? What happens when men base their self-worth primarily on what they accomplish through physical capabilities?

4. Do you think most men find it easy to do the following? Why or why not?

   a. accept the reality of diminishing health, aging, and/or sickness (see 2 Cor. 4:16; Jer. 17:5)

   b. receive the benefits of aging—greater spiritual maturity (2 Cor. 4:16–17; Jer. 90:23–24); greater wisdom; greater reliance on God's strength (1 Cor. 1:25)

Reflections for the Husband

1. How successfully have you recognized your health-related issues? Are you seeking your wife's counsel in this area?

2. What excuses have you offered for not doing what you need to do for your body?

3. What health-related changes might you need to make? Which step(s) might you start implementing this week to get yourself in better shape?

Reflections for the Wife

1. How might you use what you've read in this chapter to encourage your husband in positive ways to take better care of himself?

2. What can you learn from previous discussions with your husband that will help him face health-related issues honestly?

3. In which way(s) are you modeling what is involved in facing health concerns honestly?

4. In which way(s) might you also be in denial concerning your own health? (Be honest!)

LIE 7

1. What are some of the real reasons why many men struggle to ask for help of any kind? Why do they hold things inside—even from people who know them the best?

2. How do wives feel when their husbands won't seek help and discuss personal needs? Why do wives feel this way? What barriers do their husbands create by doing this—by accident or deliberately?

3. What can we learn—about ourselves, other people, God—when we ask for help? What effect(s) can asking for help have on our character?

4. Consider your strengths and weaknesses honestly. How might others, including your spouse, help you to shore up areas of weakness? To further strengthen your areas of strength?

5. When we recognize our need for help and then ask for it, how does that affect our relationships? How do we benefit from helping one another?

6. Do you think that each of us wants to be needed by other people? Why or why not?

Reflections for the Husband

1. How honest are you at communicating your needs with your wife? With others around you? In what way(s) might you be denying your wife a chance to express her love to you through helping?

2. What keeps you from communicating your personal needs more easily? Which step(s) might you take to improve in this area?

3. Reread the ten benefits of marriage in this chapter, then reflect on ways in which you can enable your wife truly to be your companion and helper, the one who can come alongside you and make you better and stronger.

Reflections for the Wife

1. How often do you pray for your husband and ask God to reveal ways in which you can demonstrate your love for him in practical ways?

2. Looking back over your marriage so far, how willing have you been to come alongside your husband and encourage him to ask for help?

3. To what extent have you allowed past negative experiences with your husband's pride and self-sufficiency to color your response to him today?

4. How might you help him recognize your desire to be his "help-mate" and begin to open up more about his needs?

LIE 8

1. In the introductory story, how do you think Matt felt when he returned late for the birthday party? What, if anything, might he have done to deal with the situation more effectively? Was Dana correct in asking Matt for more of his companionship, time, and interest? Why or why not?

2. What happens when a person like Matt uses his work to shore up his low self-esteem? Why is working such long hours seemingly so rewarding? Why do many men get self-worth from their accomplishments rather than from relationships?

3. Read Ecclesiastes 6:3; 2 Corinthians 9:6-11; Luke 12:13-21; Hebrews 13:5; and Proverbs 23:4-5. What are the benefits and dangers of accumulating "stuff"? Why is materialism so seductive? What is the difference between *needs* and *wants*? Why is sharing what we have so important?

4. What causes many of us (women included) to put more emphasis on *doing* than on *being*?

5. According to the authors, what is "biblical self-worth"—and where does it come from? (Consider 1 Cor. 12:7-31; Gen. 1:26-27; John 3:16)

6. What do each of the following verses reveal to us as we seek to recognize our unique giftedness and keep our self-appraisals in perspective?

   a. Romans 12:3

   b. Galatians 6:3-5

Reflections for the Husband and Wife to Read Separately

1. What did you think about and feel as you read this chapter? Why?

2. Which work-related challenges are you facing?

3. What are your real motivations for working—the attitudes, the goals, the emotions?

4. Are you willing to set aside time to talk honestly about your career(s) and related concerns and needs? If so, when will you do that? If not, why not?

5. In which area(s) might God want you to rethink job and family priorities? Be specific! Which parameters—flexible ones and those that will remain no matter what—do you think will prove helpful in charting new directions, evaluating options, and

making hard decisions concerning your work, family, and overall goals and objectives?

Lie 9

1. Why do you think Gerardo continued to avoid difficult issues even after Mimi's patient but persistent reminders? How did his actions affect their relationship?

2. What's the difference between saying "I'm sorry" and being truly repentant?

3. What causes a husband (or a wife) to *really* act differently instead of deflecting hurtful issues by making insincere statements?

4. Do you agree or disagree with this statement: "Every marriage will have conflict"? Why or why not?

5. What are some symptoms of marital disharmony? Why is it important for you and your spouse to acknowledge conflict and get issues resolved between yourselves in a frank manner, even though that will definitely increase temporary difficulties?

6. What are the risks and benefits of acknowledging the full truth about yourself to yourself? To God? To your spouse? Why is acknowledging truth so important to your family? To the body of Christ?

Reflections for the Husband

1. In what way(s) might the following influence your marriage? And if they are present, what will you do to face them? To work together with your wife to address issues honestly and make necessary changes?

    a. avoidance of conflict rather than dealing with root issues

b. avoidance of sincere, full confession when you are wrong

c. avoidance of necessary changes in your behavior

2. Read Matthew 21:28-31. Why aren't words uttered to deflect conflict and avoid changing behavior enough in the long run?

Reflections for the Wife

1. In what way(s) might the following influence your marriage? And if they are present, what will you do to face them? To work together with your husband to address issues honestly and make necessary changes?

    a. avoidance of conflict rather than dealing with root issues

    b. avoidance of sincere, full confession when you are wrong

    c. avoidance of necessary change in your behavior

2. What practical things can you do to encourage your husband to resolve issues with you truthfully, in deed and not just in word?

3. How can you avoid letting negative emotions build up if your husband continues to deflect issues and not take appropriate action?

Lie 10

1. Why is it that typical husbands tend to give their wives unsolicited advice (solutions) when the wives really want their husbands to provide emotional support (relationship) instead?

2. How do wives working through problems feel when their husbands try to give unsolicited advice in order to "fix" things? Why?

3. What are some practical ways in which husbands can provide (and show) their wives *comfort, support,* and *understanding?*

4. Why is it important for men not only to realize that they listen differently from women but to recognize the listening trait they typically neglect?

5. What are the three components of active listening? Why is each important?

6. What do you think this phrase means: "Comfort your spouse with your presence"? How does it relate to the lie mentioned in this chapter?

Reflections for the Husband

1. What can you do to train yourself to provide your wife with more emotional support when she is working through a problem?

2. Having read about the dimensions of listening, which one(s) do you typically neglect? Why? What can you do to improve in this area (and thus improve your marriage)?

3. Which of the four tips on giving advice stood out to you? Why?

4. Would you say that you are the type of friend to your wife that Proverbs 17:17 describes? Why or why not?

Reflections for the Wife

1. What can you do to guide your husband into providing you with more emotional support when you mention a problem?

2. Having read about the dimensions of listening, in which area(s) could your husband improve? What can you do to encourage him to do better?

3. Would you say that you open up to your husband, feeling safe enough to share real feelings and difficulties? If so, what does he do that provides that safety? If not, how might you guide him to practice some of the tips in this chapter?

LIE 11

1. What are the benefits—real or perceived—that make lying (or at least hiding the truth by keeping secrets) attractive to the secret keeper? On a deeper level, what are the real reasons why people keep secrets?

2. Think about secret keeping—how it has affected your life and/or the lives of people you know. Describe the consequences that occurred.

3. What are the deepest consequences of secret keeping in a marriage?

4. In which of the following areas has secret keeping occurred in your marriage or the family in which you grew up? Which small or large steps caused the secret keeping to occur?

   a. finances?

   b. accomplishments?

   c. attraction to other women (or men)?

   d. activities?

   e. wrongs?

   f. health issues?

5. What's the relationship between transparency and trust? What's at risk when a spouse discloses the truth?

6. According to Hebrews 4:12-13, why should this issue of keeping secrets be important to us today?

7. Why are grace and forgiveness so important as you and your spouse move into transparency?

Reflections for the Husband and Wife to Read Separately

1. When are you tempted to keep secrets from your spouse? Why?

2. If you are keeping secrets right now, what do you plan to do about them? What is the cost of continuing to keep secrets—to yourself, to your spouse, to others? In light of this chapter, what might you begin revealing? What can you do to avoid deceit from now on?

3. What are the dangers of true disclosure? Why, according to the authors, is true disclosure between spouses ultimately worth the risk? Why is becoming transparent with your spouse an ongoing process?

4. Respond to this: "In marriage, we should work toward eliminating anything that keeps our mate from seeing us as we really are." Do you agree or disagree? Why?

5. What can both of you do to build a safe environment that enhances openness? How might DeVito's four guidelines assist in responding to your spouse's disclosure?

6. As you restore your relationship, or strengthen it, how can you deal with negative issues in order to eliminate them from your future?

Lie 12

1. Which responses on the part of Karla and Ralph contributed to their escalating problems concerning finances?

2. Why do we sometimes try to divert or deny an issue in our marriage, thus escaping the truth about our less-than-perfect behavior?

3. What might have happened if, during the premarital counseling, Ralph had not agreed to be completely responsible for handling family finances? Which alternative options existed?

4. Read Proverbs 19:13; 21:9. Although these particular verses focus on the wife, why does nagging by either spouse backfire? What's the alternative to nagging?

5. Did the authors' perspectives on confrontation surprise you? Why or why not?

Reflections for the Husband and Wife to Read Separately

1. In which area(s) do you resist changing behavior that is negatively impacting your spouse? What's the real reason(s) for your resistance?

2. How might you begin to implement steps of accountability in your marriage?

3. Why can confrontation resulting from accountability be healing rather than damaging? What do you think the authors meant when they used the term *care-frontation*?

The Word at Work Around the World

A vital part of Cook Communications Ministries is our international outreach, Cook Communications Ministries International (CCMI). Your purchase of this book, and of other books and Christian-growth products from Cook, enables CCMI to provide Bibles and Christian literature to people in more than 150 languages in 65 countries.

Cook Communications Ministries is a not-for-profit, self-supporting organization. Revenues from sales of our books, Bible curricula, and other church and home products not only fund our U.S. ministry, but also fund our CCMI ministry around the world. One hundred percent of donations to CCMI go to our international literature programs.

CCMI reaches out internationally in three ways:

· Our premier International Christian Publishing Institute (ICPI) trains leaders from nationally led publishing houses around the world.

· We provide literature for pastors, evangelists, and Christian workers in their national language.

· We reach people at risk—refugees, AIDS victims, street children, and famine victims—with God's Word.

Word Power, God's Power

Faith Kidz, RiverOak, Honor, Life Journey, Victor, NexGen — every time you purchase a book produced by Cook Communications Ministries, you not only meet a vital personal need in your life or in the life of someone you love, but you're also a part of ministering to José in Colombia, Humberto in Chile, Gousa in India, or Lidiane in Brazil. You help make it possible for a pastor in China, a child in Peru, or a mother in West Africa to enjoy a life-changing book. And because you helped, children and adults around the world are learning God's Word and walking in his ways.

Thank you for your partnership in helping to disciple the world. May God bless you with the power of his Word in your life.

For more information about our international ministries, visit www.ccmi.org.

Additional copies of
TWELVE LIES HUSBANDS TELL THEIR WIVES
and other Life Journey titles
are available from your local bookseller.

✠ ✠ ✠

If you have enjoyed this book,
or if it has had an impact on your life,
we would like to hear from you.

Please contact us at:

LIFE JOURNEY
Cook Communications Ministries, Dept. 201
4050 Lee Vance View
Colorado Springs, CO 80918
Or at our Web site: www.cookministries.com
Or at the author's Web site: www.timriter.com

LIFE JOURNEY®
Bringing Home the Message for Life